"For more than a quarter of a century I have taught leadership. Along the journey I have met tens of thousands of leaders. Beverly Sallee Ophoff is one of the best. Her book provides principles that will help you reach your dreams."—*John Maxwell; Inc. Magazine named John C. Maxwell as the most popular leadership and management expert in the world (2014)*

"In *A Woman's Guide to 'Bootstrapping' a Business,* Beverly Sallee Ophoff shares the steps she followed to create great success in not only her life, but the lives of millions of others. She is proof positive that one person can change the world!" —*Sharon Lechter: CPA, CGMA, Author of* Think and Grow Rich for Women; *Co-author of* Rich Dad, Poor Dad; *Founder and CEO of Pay Your Family First*

"Though I knew Bev from attending the same church in Oregon, I really came to know her through conversations with widows in Rwanda who testified of her love and generosity in supporting the construction of their 'village of hope' community center. Bev is not only a successful entrepreneur, but a generous and caring leader who gives sacrificially to see others succeed." —*Dan Brose, Africa Regional Director, World Relief*

"No matter where you are, no matter who you are, you have the choice of a beautiful journey ahead of you. *A Woman's Guide to 'Bootstrapping' a Business* is a blessing to everyone who knows they were born to do more, because it really is your time."—*Diane Kennedy, CPA,* New York Times *Bestselling Author* of Loopholes of the Rich *and* Real Estate Loopholes

"Beverly Sallee Ophoff is one of our closest friends. She has been, for a long time, an important member of the Oregon Festival Chorus. She learned to experience, for herself, how music can build bridges. In later years she has made it possible for young people from different countries to attend workshops and classes at the Oregon Bach Festival. These young people came from nations with difficult political situations as Eastern Europe, Latin America, and Asia. Beverly's help made it possible for them to gain important artistic insights and establish international relationships. This proved to be essential for their future careers." —*Helmuth Rilling, Internationally known German choral conductor, founder of the Gaechinger Kantorei, the Bach-Collegium Stuttgart, the Oregon Bach Festival, Internationale Bachakademie Stuttgart*

"The lessons Beverly Sallee Ophoff shares on how to grow a business have been proven by her own tremendous financial success. She's also one of only a handful of businesswomen or men I've met who explicitly check every decision against deep-seated values—values that extend to her wide-ranging charitable work. This book shows you not just how to be prosperous in business, but how to do so without sacrificing the best in yourself." —*David Freeman, Screen Writer for Fox Television and author of* Use Hollywood Storytelling Secrets to Create Compelling Brands.

A Woman's
Guide to
BOOTSTRAPPING*
a Business

Beverly Sallee Ophoff

*BOOTSTRAPPING: AN ENTREPRENEUR
STARTING A COMPANY WITH VERY LITTLE CAPITAL

PTC
PREMIERE
TRAINING
CONCEPTS

Quotations are drawn from a number of sources, including:
Women Know Everything by Karen Weekes
Motivational Quotes by Laura Moneur
GoodReads.com
BrainyQuote.com
ThinkExist.com

ISBN 978-0-578-16143-3

Premiere Training Concepts, 2660 N. E. Hwy. 20, Ste. 610, PMB 28, Bend, OR 97701

Cover & chapter title pages by petersondesign@cox.net
Interior design by starrclay@comcast.net
Back cover photo by studio404photography.com.

TO

My dear husband, Arthur, who encouraged, helped with,
and insisted I write this book.
He has been my champion and cheerleader.
I am very grateful.
I would like to say thanks to Nick Lai from China who first
encouraged me to write a book about women in business. He
translated my other books into Mandarin several years ago. Nick
died earlier this year after running in a marathon. He is greatly
missed. I trust this book will be a tribute to him who was so
encouraging to me. My love to his family at this time.
I also thank all my dear girlfriends and notable women who
took the time to answer my interview questions.
They have been honest and transparent. I love them dearly.
I trust you, the reader, will be helped and
blessed by the stories of the actual experiences
of women in our time who are making a difference.

Know this. You can make a difference, too, if you WILL.
I am cheering for you.

PREFACE

She Has Lived It!

Beverly has lived successfully the things she has spoken about and written here in spite of many times of duress. She was a career musician until 1978 when she started a business of her own on the side. She has helped establish businesses for many people around the world from all walks of life. In my opinion, her best work has been in the international arena. The values that permeate her business remain the same whether in the United States of America or any other nation around the world where she has gone. She continues to provide leadership training for a strong and influential team of her business associates.

Beverly counsels members of her groups about how to address family issues, and issues arising from husband-wife being equal partners, which is a foreign concept in a large part of our world. She has a heart for the single woman who often feels powerless to change her situation. This book was written with these women in mind: the woman who needs encouragement in a business she is attempting to establish, a woman who believes her business may have global impact, any woman in need of a meaningful business to augment her income and convey her talents to the world, and perhaps especially, the woman who feels powerless to change her situation in life, or to become financially successful.

Through owning a business many relationships are formed that last a lifetime. Beverly gives both testament and counsel to all these.

This book may be what you have been looking for!

—Dr. Arthur Ophoff

Up by the Bootstraps

From the time I was a child I wanted to be on stage, and eventually I was—as a speaker, not an actress. Getting from where I was born to that stage wasn't at all easy. My family had little money and I knew from an early age that I would have to work hard to achieve any kind of success.

I had to pull myself up by the bootstraps.

I studied hard in school and got a tuition scholarship to college. I labored through difficult jobs to pay the other expenses at college—from bussing dishes in the dining hall to assisting the professors in directing school musicals.

I had no time to date or go to football games.

After graduating from college I got a job as a speech and English teacher for thirty-five dollars a week. On the side, I also taught charm courses to women, which led eventually to my becoming a motivational speaker and author of forty books.

It was at this point that I met Beverly. I was preparing to speak at a business convention when my host took me backstage to the green room. As I entered I heard the voice of a very tall elegant woman.

"Who is that?" I asked my host.

With a whispering almost-reverent tone she said, "That's our leader. We all wish to be like Beverly."

There she stood—with her head above the clouds, her laugh contagious, and her chiffon sleeves waving in the breezes. In every way, she was "above" her audience. Draped in a column of sequined sparkles, she was both statuesque and stunning.

As the crowd parted to make a path for me, I approached her and said, "Anyone who can wear a white fringed gown at lunch time is someone I have got to know!"

I did get to know Beverly as a dear friend. We mentored each other in a number of ways. I was grateful to learn her principles of successful leadership, which she is generously sharing with you in this book.

You may not be as tall as Beverly, but you can learn from her how to be a leader of people who will look up to you.

Now is your time.

— Florence Littauer

Contents

Contents

CHAPTER 1

Define Yourself

*BOOTSTRAPPING:
AN ENTREPRENEUR
STARTING A COMPANY
WITH VERY LITTLE CAPITAL

"Life is a verb, not a noun."

Charlotte Perkins Gilman (1860–1935)
American Writer and Social Critic

This IS for you. My story is told so that YOU might believe your life can be different. You CAN own your future.

Eleanor Roosevelt said, "In the long run, we shape our lives, and we shape ourselves. The process never ends until we die. And the choices we make are ultimately our own responsibility." She is also quoted as saying, "No one can make you feel inferior without your consent." (Eleanor Roosevelt 1884–1962, American First Lady and Political Leader)

My purse was stolen while I was in London. In a little more than an instant, I *felt inferior.* In other words, helpless and without an identity! No passport, no money or credit cards, no phone, no way of proving that I was who I said I was!

It was a strange feeling for me suddenly to be without resources, or definition. I had *nothing.*

But wait … I was with family and friends! And that meant I had everything.

My friends paid the bill at the hotel. My son Paul identified me at the U.S. Embassy so I could get another passport. My friend Derek drove us to the airport.

Eleanor Roosevelt's statement has a key word in it: FEEL. You are *not* inferior unless you convince yourself that you are. You may "feel" inferior at times, but wake up and let go of that feeling! In truth, you are not inferior … not now, not ever.

At the outset of this book, I also have some terms to define for you, just to make sure we are on the same page:

- *Duress*—threats, violence, constraint, or other actions brought to bear on someone to do something against their will or better judgment.
- *Success*—the accomplishment of an aim or purpose.

And here are some important "in" words for you to know:

- *Innate*—arising from birth, originating in the constitution of the mind rather than learned through experience.
- *Inherent*—existing in something as a permanent, essential, or characteristic attribute.
- *Inviolable*—too important to be ignored or treated with disrespect.
- *Inalienable*—not tranferrable to another or capable of being repudiated. [*Merriam-Webster Dictionary*]

It is time for you to define yourself! Take stock of who you are inside and build on that for your future.

There are many women today who lament the fact that they were never given the opportunity to have a business for themselves. Now is the time to remedy that.

Women are still on the rise in earning equal pay for equal work. They are still gaining a strong and stronger foothold in some professions. They are still attempting to break the "crystal ceiling" in many corporations and international conglomerates. And they are still pioneering one specific aspect of the business world: *entrepreneurship.*

Women are starting new businesses in record numbers, but they are still a long way from having widespread accomplishment and recognition as small-business owners (on their way to becoming large-business owners). As part of this trend, they are still struggling *within themselves* over whether they can be as successful as men in business, can lead in the business realm as well as men, and can influence others to follow in their wake and become even *greater* in financial wealth and organizational success. Furthermore, what is true for women in the United States of America is even *more* true for women in other nations, and especially the developing nations.

If any of the preceding paragraph rings true for you, this book is for *YOU.*

I have now been in business for more than thirty-six years, and have been part of founding and leading business groups in many nations. Business is not my *total* life, but hear me closely on this:

Business IS a key to what makes my life *whole*.

Being in business has made my *whole* life more enriching, more meaningful, and more exciting.

If that is appealing to you, then this book is also for *YOU*.

When I first started in business some of my colleagues at the university would say to me, "Beverly, what is a professional musician doing in commerce?" The general perception was that business was a rather ruthless, cut-throat activity, especially entrepreneurial ventures or start-up enterprises. Also, it was viewed as a man's world—and men didn't always play fair and certainly weren't going to go out of their way to help, mentor, or financially back a woman, as a rule.

I had a very different opinion. I held on to a different dream. Usually, I listened and smiled and kept my ideas to myself. It is best to be quiet and work rather than brag about what you are going to do. Just do it! They will catch on.

I knew why a college professor with a master's degree in music was going into business. I was broke! I needed money for many things.

How about you?

My Early Years Set Me on the Path

I didn't grow up rich. In fact, you couldn't see rich out my back door. In fact, for many of my growing-up years you couldn't even see much that you might have labeled "civilization"! It wasn't that we lived among savages or were like savages. The local people were nice, good-hearted, generous people for the most part. But, they were all just as poor as we were. And we were *poor*.

As a child, I knew we were poor but because so many around me were poor, I didn't have much stigma attached to poverty. It just meant not having *AS MUCH MONEY* as I hoped to have some day.

There's an old *Dennis the Menace* cartoon to which I have always related well. Dennis is sitting in his chair, facing the corner of a room as a punishment for a bit of mischief. He says, "I may be sitting down on the outside, but I'm standing up on the inside." That was always the attitude I had, even as a young child.

According to my parents, I had a deeply stubborn streak.

My mother told me that, as a little girl, I would go out each morning to the small pasture by our house and square off with our goat. He would knock me over. I would get up and he would knock me over again. Stubborn, unwilling to give up, I was standing up on the *inside*!

One of the advantages of having ambition and a strong will is that you aren't easily bowled over by small or even average-sized problems. You outsmart, outrun, or out-maneuver those problems. You aren't dismayed by people who make fun of you or ignore you or reject you. You walk on with your head high. And, you don't take kindly to people who say they "can't" or "won't." You assure them they can and will, or you "won't."

Meet Jules

I draw great encouragement from my friend Jules.

She was raised by her single mom as her father was in a mental hospital for most of her life.

Jules remembers at age five striving to run from her nightmare of struggle, and driving to succeed and prove her worth through accomplishments. This inner "drive" produced the motivation and the strength that led to her graduating from high school at the age of sixteen. She was on a path to attend college early, but at age seventeen, she had a tragic car accident, which diverted her path to months of hospitalizations and rehab. At age twenty, she went into business for herself and has become successful in many ways.

All along the way, Jules never quit! She never let family or physical circumstances dictate her outcomes.

When I was fourteen years old, my father sold everything we owned and bought a dairy farm. He had some experience in farming, but little experience in the dairy business. Still, it was his dream to be a dairy farmer. I am glad he pursued his dream, even though it didn't work out too well.

During the year, my mother became ill and we needed to move. My younger sister and I took over all of the household chores—the cooking, cleaning, ironing, and everything else that went with the running of a home. We also helped my dad in the dairy, getting up before school every morning and stripping the forty cows after they had been milked with an electric milker and doing some of the chores that went along with that operation.

The sad news is that the price of milk dropped dramatically that year and my father lost everything. We became dairy farmers quickly … and we were out of business in one year. I was fourteen and Dad said to me, "You need to get a driver's license, right away." In Texas a fourteen-year-old who was helping out on a farm could get a driver's license. So I quickly learned how to drive a stick-shift truck out in the pasture. I navigated my way through a few holes and ditches but eventually learned how to drive that truck with a reasonable degree of skill. And then Dad said, "You're going to drive the car and follow me and we're heading out in just a few days."

We drove about four hundred miles across Texas and I admit to you, I was scared every mile of that drive. I had only been driving a couple of weeks, I didn't have a map, and I didn't have any money. All I had in the car with me was my driver's license and my little dog and the command to follow the tail lights on my dad's truck. More than once we got to an intersection and Dad made the light and I didn't. What to do? I didn't know whether to turn, and if so, in which direction. Fortunately, Dad was always waiting for me at the edge of town.

That experience was one of the greatest lessons in trust that I have ever been "taught."

Our new home was just north of Houston and Dad hired two men to unload the truck and he went to a new job and left the house for my sister and me to "set up." I was in charge of telling the moving guys where to put what, and then I went to the school the next day and enrolled myself and my sister Barbara.

Did I think that I was experiencing tremendous struggles or hardships during those months and years?

No. I saw this as "just life."

Some things were difficult.

Some things were new challenges.

Some things were a little scary.

But I never once thought that life was supposed to be handed to me on any kind of platter, much less a silver platter. Life was to be faced and *conquered*. And I saw myself as a good candidate for "conqueror!"

I learned very early in life what it means to "roll with it" and to be flexible and make adjustments—and to face rough times with courage and then to enjoy the good times with an all-embracing enthusiasm.

During the years that my father was working as a builder, my sister and I helped carry bricks and stir up cement for building projects related to our own home. We nailed up laths for lath-and-plaster wall coverings when we were in the third and fourth grades. We *worked*, and I don't think it hurt me one bit.

I was always tall for my age—no matter my age! I figured early on that if I was going to be at least six feet tall that I'd probably need to breathe twice as much air as the petite girls my age, and I automatically concluded that if I was going to be twice as tall and breathe twice as much air as other people, I needed to be twice as good at whatever I put my mind to. I knew that because I was poor, I was going to have to work twice as hard to earn my way, just to get to average. I became extremely performance oriented.

In third grade, the school held a reading contest. I don't remember what the prize was held out to be, but I do remember that I was determined to win it. I read thirty-five books in two weeks. I won. I always tried to win, and most of the time when I competed at something, I did win.

People who are driven to succeed like I was usually have strong heroes in their life. My father was one of my heroes. For a number of years, Dad worked as an immigration officer on the Mexican border and he had a number of dramatic experiences. I vividly recall one morning when he came home after working all night and his entire uniform was covered with blood. I took one look at him and concluded that he must be on the verge of dying.

As it turned out, my father was in the process of taking an illegal immigrant into custody when the man, who was on drugs, broke away from him and ran through a plate-glass door. He was cut up badly, but my father caught him and held on to him and wouldn't let him get away. My father told me years later that he never drew a gun in all his years of immigration-control work, but he was also fearless in capturing illegal immigrants and taking them back across the border. He had the courage to walk into situations that many people would run from.

When I was teaching high school in Pasadena, California, my father came to one of the school's football games. A large number of inner-city kids were at the game, which was held in the Rose Bowl. They began to have a gang fight and a few of the guys started roughing up a policeman. My dad, who was sixty years old at the time, walked right into that fray and said in a commanding voice, "Break it up right now. Get out of here! What do you think you're doing roughing up this cop?" He flashed his federal badge and one of the gang members said, "Hey man, he's a fed. Move out!" And they did. The fight ended. Dad never touched a person, but he was obviously in control.

Who wouldn't want a hero like my dad?

I had women I admired as well. There was one woman at church who was very tall—obviously that was an important feature to me—and beautiful and I admired her lovely singing voice and also the fact that she wore stylish shoes even though she had big feet. One day she asked me to accompany her on the organ as she sang a solo in church. I was scared nearly to the point of paralysis. What if I screwed up? What if I played in the wrong key? But she had confidence in me and I overcame my fear and basked in her appreciation, and learned a good lesson in what it means to have quiet courage in the face of fear.

Another of my heroes was a guy named Joe. I met Joe in college. He had only one arm. At age twelve, he had been riding his bicycle and got to a train crossing and fell and a train ran over his arm, severing it. That didn't stop him from becoming a fantastic trumpet player. His false arm was outfitted with a hook, and he used that to hold his trumpet, as he manipulated the keys with his other hand. He was also number-two on the tennis team! When he served, he tossed the ball and then grabbed his racket with the same arm to hit the ball. He was amazing to watch. We became good friends, and I watched Joe struggle his way through many things. We traveled together on a choir tour sponsored by the college and at every stop on the way, Joe found himself being stared at by a new group of young people. He took it all in stride and he'd tease those who gawked at him, saying, "What, you guys never seen Captain Hook?" And he'd let them touch his hook, and answer their questions about it.

I am amused when people say to me that they are "scared" to give a presentation to a group of six or eight people, knowing they have a flip chart and printed booklet that makes it all easily doable. Joe had to live with fear and the potential of being laughed at every day of his teenage and adult life!

I once took about thirty-five girls to a choir event at a hospital in San Francisco. The children at that hospital were there because they had either a terminal disease or an extreme physical handicap. I saw the eyes of my choir students get as big as saucers. It was the first encounter many of them had ever had with people who truly had to struggle just to live through another day.

I had told my choir in advance, "Whatever you do, do not cry. Cry later. You are here today to give these children something to smile about and to create a happy memory for them." They did what I asked.

One of the girls, a big "tough girl" named Vicki—who was our drummer and had aspirations of becoming a police officer—may have had a hard shell on the outside, but she had a soft heart. She melted that day when she encountered a beautiful, young, dark-skinned boy about six years old who had no arms, and only two little hooks coming out of his shoulder sockets. Vicki went to him and put her two drumsticks into his hooks and showed him how to play her drum.

We gathered around the children and sang "It's a Small World After All," as he kept the beat for us with his drumsticks. The look on his face was as priceless as the look in Vicki's eyes.

I have rarely been as proud of a student as I was of Vicki that day. She gave that little boy something to believe in, hope for, and dream about. He told her, "I'm going to be a drummer when I grow up." She replied, "You can be!" It was as if they had signed a contract to make it so.

In many ways, when I give a person an opportunity to become a small-business owner—with a plan to follow and products that are great for her to sell—I feel as if I am putting drumsticks into the hands of a person who has not had *anything* to hold onto or to use for greater success in their lives.

I have seen this in America, and to an even more profound extent overseas. Most of us in America do not comprehend the depth and breadth of the pain and struggle that many people in the world experience, not just "on occasion" but as the norm of life.

My Love for Music Gave Me Focus

When my sister and I were toddlers we moved to the border of Texas and Mexico, where my father had a job as a border patrol inspector. Barbara and I were the only Caucasian girls in town, and the only English-speaking ones, it seemed. One day I sneaked out the back door of our home, went to the neighbor's house, and opened their door. I got under the sink and into their black shoe polish and made myself a darker shade and then I walked into their parlor and banged on their piano. The neighbor woman thought it was wonderful that I had musical and theatrical talent!

My mother was horrified, but she also recognized that I had a great love for the piano. When I was nine, we were living in a larger town and my mother arranged for me to take piano lessons. We didn't have the money to pay for the lessons after a while, so my mother painted the music teacher's house in exchange for lessons. I was very grateful, and still am, for that opportunity.

And, by the way, I am grateful my mother "displayed" another great principle that became important to me through the years—a barter can be just as good as a cash exchange.

I went on to study piano in college and as a piano major, earned a Bachelor of Arts degree.

In my teens and early twenties, I had a dream of being a concert pianist—of playing beautiful grand pianos all around the world. I practiced long and hard to develop my piano-playing skills. In high school, I played for the military officers at their cocktail parties making five dollars an hour, which was good money for a teenager in those days! When I was in college, I played the organ at a church for twenty-five dollars a week.

I saw music as a wonderful privilege and as a great money-making career. I didn't know how few and far those privileges might be.

Why I Left Teaching

Through the years, people have said to me on occasion, "Teaching wasn't such a bad life, was it?" They often add with a little chuckle, "After all, teachers get off June, July, and August."

I reply that I truly did enjoy teaching. I had a good time with the students, and I believe that I did good work in teaching students how to read music, perform music, and enjoy music. I also had opportunities to earn extra money in the summer months teaching summer school music classes.

So why did I choose to leave teaching?

Let me make it clear that I did not leave teaching "cold turkey." I didn't go from being a full-time music professor at a local college to being a full-time business woman. I made a gradual, albeit fairly fast, transition from one full-time job to the other.

All the years I was teaching, I never knew a teacher who didn't have both a teaching job and at least some kind of secondary job.

I had a number of secondary jobs through the years. I taught private music lessons—mostly piano but also voice. I helped with choirs for various community performances and Broadway-style shows. I also helped pick and preserve fruits and vegetables to help the family budget.

After nine years of teaching and nine years of "summers off," I felt that I had pretty much "been there, done that."

The Ongoing Need

When I first moved to Bend, Oregon, I thought the area was very beautiful, but since I didn't have a job when we first moved there, I didn't have any money to spend for things we needed or wanted. I heard some people talk about canning "over in the valley" and I was too embarrassed to ask exactly where to go or what to look for. I just headed over the mountain and found a roadside stand and said to the woman there, "I want to make pickles."

The woman running the stand asked me if I wanted to make gherkins, bread and butter, sweet and sour, or 21-day pickles. I didn't know the difference, so I walked away in embarrassment. I realized I didn't know anything about pickles. I also didn't know anything about living a rural life, or the first thing about making something that I might be able to sell in my *own* roadside stand!

My need for money came down to a very basic realization: I needed *more* money than the amount of money I had. More specifically, I had a need for more money than I later was making in my regular "salaried" position. There were things I needed to buy that didn't fit my budget— unexpected uniforms for a child in sports, music lessons that I considered a "must" for my children, braces for teeth that needed braces, and so forth.

I took a look at the world as a whole and came to a conclusion that when most people need money, they *sell* something.

I thought, "What do I have to sell?"

I could have sold our television set, or the children's rocking horse that they were now too big to ride anyway. I watched people around me hold "garage" sales on the driveway leading up to their garage.

Selling *something* is the way that most people make money when they need a little more money than what they make in their "day job."

I did a little research and decided that I just might be able to sell products for a particular company and make the extra money I needed.

Mind you, I didn't feel the need for a *lot* of money. I just wanted about three hundred dollars a month *more* money than what I was already earning "on the job." That factored out to about seventy-five dollars a week, and I thought, "Surely I can sell something that will add up to seventy-five dollars a week."

Well, surely I *could.*

And surely, just about any person I know *can*, too.

CHAPTER 2

Launching Out

BOOTSTRAPPING:
AN ENTREPRENEUR
STARTING A COMPANY
WITH VERY LITTLE CAPITAL

"If you're never scared or embarrassed or

hurt, it means you never take any chances."

Julia Sorel (pen name for Rosalyn Drexler) (1926–)
Pop Artist, Novelist, Emmy-Award Winning Screenplay Writer

When I was a young teenager, our family went to Acapulco, Mexico, on a vacation. The owner of the hotel where we stayed had a son who had access to a speedboat. One afternoon we were at the beach and this young man and his friend boated over to where we were lying on a beach. The young man jumped out of the boat and swam over to us and asked my sister and me to go for a ride. My father gave our answer for us, an adamant NO. (I don't think he even added a "gracias" to the "no.")

My sister and I were very upset—Dad had just kept us from a ride in a speedboat with two older guys.

We didn't see any dangers in the invitation—no danger related to the two older guys, no danger related to the boat. But Dad knew.

And many times down through the years, both my sister and I thanked him for his wisdom that kept us safe.

It is true, of course, that neither my sister nor I may have come to harm that day. BUT ... there was a risk of something going wrong that was too great for Dad to take.

My father had a keen insight into the motives and character of people. He saw no potential good in his young daughters being whisked away in a speedboat with two men significantly older than his girls.

Dad also knew that the kidnapping of young American girls was becoming more widespread in the area where we were staying. He wasn't interested in seeing his daughters hurt emotionally, wounded in a boating accident, or *kidnapped*.

He weighed the opportunity for us to have a fun time and decided the answer was "no way."

I always encourage those who are seeking a business of their own, or who are considering joining me in my business endeavors, to weigh very carefully the options before them.

All Choices Have Consequences

Choices are always connected to consequences. Every person needs to weigh both about every major life decision.

Just because someone wants you to do something doesn't mean you *should* do it.

I once let someone talk me into riding a motorcycle. I wasn't all that excited about the idea but I got on the motorcycle to please this person. There were several immediate warning signs that this wasn't a good idea for me.

First, a dog bit me on the leg while I was stopped at a red light. Then, while riding in the mountains, a rock came sliding off a mountain and hit me in the face, breaking my sunglasses and causing me to have a bloody nose.

Later, I had an accident in the desert while riding in deep sand, and I broke my leg. I had a four-month old baby at the time—a friend was watching my child. It is a bad idea to have an infant and a shattered leg at the same time. It took me seven months to walk again, and in the end, my baby and I both were learning to "walk" at the same time!

Through the years, I had to have a number of surgeries on this leg and finally a knee replacement. One bad decision on my part led to years of pain. Yes, riding a motorcycle had its moments of exhilarating open-air fun, but "fun" is never the only consequence of a choice!

That's wisdom for all "opportunities" that we are given in which any kind of risk is involved. Don't buy into something—mentally and emotionally, or with money—just because it holds out the promise of reward or a future lifestyle that is fun and exciting. Never enter a business just because somebody else may think it is a good idea for you to do so!

The decision needs to be *your* decision, and one you weigh with caution.

Weigh ALL that is involved in that opportunity very carefully. Don't get into anything on a whim.

Consider the time and effort involved.

Consider your desire to put out a great deal of effort.

Consider *not* how you will sell your first thousand units of something, but how you will begin to sell the first hundred units. Consider *not* how many millions of dollars you might make, but how you are going to earn your first five hundred dollars.

And, always consider the "worst-case" scenario. Most mature adults can imagine a worst-case scenario … and if the worst-case scenario is not one that you would want an innocent and beloved child of yours to experience … don't take the risk.

"But," you may be sputtering, "that eliminates just about everything in life!"

No, not really.

Life has *countless* risks that *may* result in the potential for minor loss, and yet not produce major catastrophe. Many of those risks have potential for some gain.

The tendency is for big-risk opportunities to hold out massive gains, which are not at all realistic. Massive gains are possible in life, but usually as the result of long, arduous, persevering *work* that is consistent and steady.

I do not say any of this to be discouraging. Rather, realistic.

The most realistic thing you can do at the outset is to identify your own "excuses" for *not* going into business for yourself. The truth is, there are many *good* reasons for going into business—far more than the number of negative reasons, in my opinion. But, many people get hung up on the potential bad outcomes and never explore the good potential outcomes! "Focusing on the negative" is usually another way of saying, "making an excuse." There's never anything good coming out of a motivation rooted in excuses. Facts, yes. Excuses, no.

Meet Maria

My friend Maria certainly *could* have used excuses for not launching her own business.

Maria grew up on a farm in Austria and in her words, "was always very ambitious." At age fifteen, she was on the Austrian national ski team and was a professional ski racer. She experienced a number of injuries and eventually resigned from the team to become a certified massage therapist, working in two large hotels. At the time she entered her own marketing business, she had four major responsibilities: her massage practice, two children, managing a large apartment building, and a business in the tourism industry conducting exercise classes as a certified coach in the Tyrolean Alps three times a week.

Maria openly admits that her biggest obstacle to success was her own negative outlook on life. It was her marketing job opportunity that gave her a more positive, open-minded perspective, and turned her into the self-confident person she is today. She is able to give a seminar in front of ten thousand people, impromptu … now, that's *confidence*!

In the early days of her marketing business, she also learned the lessons of "hard work" and "perseverance." She once presented her product line eighty-five times in a row without one sale. Even so, she persevered! And today, she has become one of the top producers in her field.

Maria is a living example to me that a woman can turn any excuse into success. If Maria could make it, you can!

Face Down Your Own Fears

If you have "toyed" with the idea of starting your own business—daydreamed about it, wondered about it, jotted down a few notes about it, had a couple of conversations about it—but haven't actually set sail on a voyage into entrepreneurship … take a long hard look at WHY.

What are the excuses you are telling yourself?

Write them down.

Are you letting your own sense of "lack" hold you back?

The excuses people use are amazing at times.

Some think they just can't succeed at a sales position if they don't have a new car. They don't believe they can show a business plan in their home because their home is too small.

Some think they need to have more money in their wallet to show others, for some strange reason, that they don't really *need* more money (when in fact, they don't want to admit that whether it's a true need or not, they *want* more money).

Some think they need a high-profile job or a stronger social standing, or a better-looking spouse, or even a better-looking dog.

I once went to the home of a couple who *could* have come up with all sorts of excuses. Neither the husband or wife looked like successful people—when it came to what they wore or the quality of items in their home. They were clean people, but not all that stylish. Their home was quite small. The living space where my presentation was scheduled to be given was large enough for a dozen people, eight of them sitting on folding chairs. But if you had looked into their master bedroom, you would have found egg crates being used for nightstands. They had an old Volkswagen bug parked in their driveway.

But ... they smiled and greeted those who came with a positive upbeat attitude and a genuine belief that *others* could succeed *even if they didn't*. They never really said they didn't think they were doomed to fail, but they *did* say often how much they thought a person who was at the meeting could not only do the business, but do *very well* in the business! They conveyed a tremendous amount of encouragement, and they also knew the facts and figures related to the business and its products and services.

Fast forward five years. You can guess the outcome. They were more stylish in their appearance. They had moved to a bigger house. They were driving a better car. And they were still hosting meetings for potential recruits, still selling product, and still working the business plan for the company they had joined. They had a strong upward trend in their business but it hadn't diminished in the least their focus on *others*, nor had it diluted the warmth of their encouragement or the genuine enthusiasm they had for their own futures and the futures of others.

What's standing in your way? It is likely your own wall of excuses. So ... what can you do to climb over that wall and get going?

I encourage those who start a new business to write down their initial fears and perceptions related to risk and failure. Do this in the first few weeks of starting your business. Lay that statement aside—where you can find it later, but don't see it all the time. And then, get busy working the plan that has been set before you to work! Do what you know to do, with diligence, persistence, and a positive outlook.

A year later, take a look at your statement about fears, failure, and risks. I have found that in ninety percent of the cases in which the person has persisted through the vicissitudes of the first year, they smile at their initial fears and negative feelings. Why? Because they have worked through them and are succeeding! The overall trend is upward, even with a few jagged downturns along the way.

Face Up to the Inevitability of Change

Have you ever had a time in your life when you wore hand-me-downs? I didn't experience this as a little girl because I was the first-born daughter, but I have a hunch my younger sister always had a little bit of resentment about receiving *my* hand-me-downs.

I certainly did have my share of hand-me-downs or second-hand "gift items" when I began to live on my own and during the early years of marriage. Some of the items given to me were in great disrepair, but I was grateful for a chair, even a broken-down chair. Some of the items had sentimental value or family history attached to them—to the point that even though I didn't *like* that lamp, I convinced myself that it gave off good light in a dark corner and I kept replacing its bulbs instead of replacing the lamp.

And then came the days when I could afford *new* things—a chair *and* a sofa and loveseat that were in good repair and covered in exquisite upholstery. I could afford matching lamps that were elegant and flooded my new living room with light. And along the way, I could afford real-wood furniture, no more particle board, and really beautiful carpets on the floor.

The items I purchased gave me pleasure and comfort, and they also sent a signal to my own mind and soul that I was a person who was *worthy* of quality. Nobody else needed to see my new furniture for *me* to experience a boost in my own sense of self-value.

My experience with new furnishings led me rather quickly to an understanding that there are many people—including the "old me"—who needed to replace some of their old ideas and prejudices, old fears, and old beliefs with NEW ideas, opinions, and beliefs. They needed to upgrade their own thinking, and their own degree of self-appreciation or self-esteem.

No adult must, or should, remain stuck in their childhood pain.

Were you ever told as a child that you were "stupid" ... or a "dunderhead" ... or that you would never amount to anything? Were you ever told that you were unlovable ... or had no value ... or could never succeed?

Do you ever feel "bad" about yourself because of what a parent, older sibling, an older relative, or any type of authoritative figure said to you or did to you when you were a child?

Are the *ideas* in that previous paragraph painful to read?

If there is anything that rings true about your own childhood experiences in what I have written above, hear this strong word from me: YOU need some new mental and emotional furniture in your mind and soul! You are not today what others said about you "back then." You can and must adopt a new appreciation for *yourself!*

If others from the "old gang" don't appreciate your current level of success, gather new friends to be your "new gang" that is supportive and encouraging and appreciative of the person you are, and are still in the process of *becoming.*

If others in your family or old neighborhood don't understand what you are doing—perhaps they've never been in business for themselves or don't know anybody who is a small-business owner— don't waste too much time trying to explain your motivations or dreams. Simply smile and say, "I'm enjoying the challenge" or, "I'm discovering new things about myself all the time." Sometimes family members and old friends have a sense that you are leaving them behind in some way. You can assure them that you are still going to be a loyal, loving daughter, sister, friend, or whatever the relationship might be.

At times, you may need to acknowledge to yourself, or even to your circle of friends and family members, that you are willing to include them in your *new* circle of friends and associates, but that you aren't going to be forced into a position of having to choose between them and your new business colleagues and team members, or the new friends you are making as you develop your business. Granted, I don't know of too many instances in which people "from the past" jumped at the idea of becoming "new recruits or trainees," or even new customers ... but if you make that offer sincerely, and they reject that offer soundly, you at least have the personal satisfaction of having done your best to hold on to your new self-value without compromise.

Very importantly, don't go to the flea market in search of your old discarded furniture! In other words, don't go looking for another person who will become a critic or demoralizer. Once you have a focus for your dreams—in this case, perhaps a business you are going to give your all to pursuing—remain firmly committed to your goals and the pursuit of your dreams, and don't let anything or anyone from your past hold you back.

Consider Others on Your Path

I am not in the least telling you that you should disregard all others who are part of your life. I do, however, encourage you to evaluate the role that others in your life may play in your unfolding future.

Have you seen the cartoon that shows two men looking across the street at a couple of businesses? One of the places has a sign that says "AA" over the door—it is a regular meeting place for Alcoholics Anonymous groups. The other place has a sign "Joe's Bar."

One of the two men says, "Hey, let's go to a meeting. It will be good for us."

The other man says, "Ok. But first, let's pop in for a drink."

We smile, because we can see how unproductive the second guy's idea would be. Even so ... how many of us do that when it comes to being around people that we *know* will bring us down, yet we agree to meet with them, party with them, or go somewhere with them because we don't want to hurt their feelings? We don't mind hurting our *own* inner balance or self-worth—we care more about what they will think of us than we care about the impact of their negative opinions on our wellbeing.

One very early morning after speaking at a major conference the night before, I found myself at an airport, sitting at a little table by a big window with a large cup of coffee in hand. I watched a 747 airplane being pulled away from an airport gate and into a good runway position by a very tiny tractor. I almost laughed out loud. It was humorous to think that this huge, gorgeous plane could be positioned by a small, nondescript, rather dirty-looking four-wheeler. But that's what was happening.

The tractor driver was in charge, not the pilot.

At the same time, I knew that as soon as the plane was unhooked from the tractor, the pilot would fire up the engines and soar into the sky.

Who is pulling you around? Who has taken charge of your thinking and believing? Is it someone who is getting you in a *good* position so that when you are untethered, you can fly?

If the person pulling you around by the nose is not eager for you to fly on your own, unhook *yourself* from that relationship. Get yourself free!

You may not need to end the *entire* relationship, but you will need to unhook the control the other person has over your material and career success if you are going to pursue a business that is going to soar.

You will need to become very proactive in putting yourself in positive places ... with positive people ... who have a positive message.

Choose which events you will attend in your life.

Choose whom you will develop as friends, colleagues, and business associates.

Choose what you will listen to, read, or watch—weigh carefully *all* that you take into your mind and heart.

Is there someone who is trying to live vicariously through your activities and your achievements? Recognize what is happening. Give words of appreciation to the person for what the person has helped you do, accomplish, or experience in the past, but don't hold back your own trajectory toward the blue sky of maximum success because another person is tied to you in any way that holds you back or keeps you down.

Your Entrance into the Business World

Through the years, I have recorded a number of informational and motivational messages that were aimed at women, and sitting in a recording studio, I found it an interesting challenge to imagine my "audience."

I got to the place where I could see clearly in my mind's eye a woman listening to me as she navigated her morning commute down a busy freeway, heading for her place of employment. I could "see" other women putting on their makeup, in a hurry to get the children fed and out the door, cleaning up the kitchen a bit, and her husband asking if she knew where he had put his car keys.

Still other women were ones I envisioned sitting down on a couch or in an easy chair, trying to relax for a few minutes between dinner and bedtime rituals, hoping to capture just a few minutes of "me" time.

For each of these women, life was no doubt a juggling act—successfully or unsuccessfully attempting to keep a job and career going and at the same time, carving out a bit of personal time to pursue personal goals … or perhaps just to breathe.

I can relate to the women in my mind because I was one of them for about twenty years. I had a full-time job, was raising a daughter and son, and was building my own business on the side. I was married for most of those years, as a friend said, "for better and worse," and most months, I was surprised in two ways at the end of a month. First, I was surprised that I was still alive and still relatively sane, and second, surprised that we were out of money … *again.*

The routine of life was usually at a breakneck speed. The bills of life were boringly repetitive—they just kept coming around, again and again. I found myself increasingly discouraged, wondering if I would ever be able to get ahead of the curve, if I would ever be able to give my children the experiences I wanted them to have, and eventually, the college education I hoped they would want. I wondered if I would ever be able to relax just a little and *enjoy* the beauty and adventure of life that I knew must be out there somewhere.

Turning on the television only made matters worse. The news is never good, and I suppose if it was, it wouldn't be "the news." The entertainment programs invariably displayed experiences and a lifestyle that I didn't have—either more violent, more glamorous, more stimulating, or more romantic, and nearly always more prosperous. Nobody on the television sitcoms, even those who were supposedly living in average neighborhoods, seemed to live in a neighborhood that was as average as mine.

It wasn't always that way for all women, of course. My aunt, Ethel, was a tremendous inspiration to me, and still is. She had worked and had established a wonderful business of her own during the Great Depression, designing "fancy" clothes for children! Her clientele was wealthy—she wasn't and my family wasn't and most of America wasn't in those days, but those who purchased from her were wealthy, and I grew up knowing what the finer things of life were like … but from afar.

Most women of Aunt Ethel's generation, however, did not have businesses of their own, and most of them did not work outside their own home. Their worries often revolved around getting the washing and ironing done, and hoping to have an adequate dinner ready by the time their husband arrived at home.

In today's world, it is *expected* that a woman will work outside the home—mostly to meet the demands in today's economy, but for many, also to validate their college degrees. In my great aunt's day, it was a luxury to meet your "girlfriends" for lunch in the department store "tea room." In my day, most of my friends did not believe they had time for a leisurely lunch, and the department stores have morphed into discount centers that have no tea rooms!

I have met literally thousands of women who are asking:

When will it be my turn?

When will I have time between dawn and dusk to think creatively, or to pursue an interest that is purely my own?

When will I have enough income to hire somebody else to run the vacuum cleaner so I can hop into my new minivan and take the kids out for a day of fun?

Do you ask yourself questions such as these? I certainly asked those questions!

In 2012 I read a set of numbers put out by the Bureau of Labor Statistics. The report said that sixty-six percent of mothers with children had full-time jobs outside the home. The median income for men was $935 a week. A woman's weekly income was $765. Sixty-two percent of working mothers said they would prefer working part-time.

According to the Office of Economic Research and the Office of Advocacy the demographics of business owners have changed little for women from 2007 to 2012. In 2007, 35.9 percent of businesses in the United States were owned by women. In 2012, thirty-six percent were owned by women.

The earning statistics are still in favor of men. Even though more women are graduating from college these days than men, men still are paid more money for doing identical jobs as women. In many cases, women must work harder to prove themselves in the corporate world, just to "win" lower positions and lower salaries.

I say: "Forget the corporate world! Own your own corporation. Control the amount of money you will make and keep. It is up to you."

At the time I made the decision to pursue a business of my own, I was a college teacher, and most of my colleagues were men. I knew that most of the men I worked alongside would have found it very difficult to have a woman as their manager or "boss" in a corporate environment. They barely tolerated women as chairmen of faculty committees and academic departments.

I had a number of friends who were struggling to motivate their husbands up the ladder of success. Many of these friends had college degrees, but they had faced the fact that their husband's job was going to be the "money" job in the family, so they did their utmost to help him succeed. They recommended the right books, encouraged him to attend the right meetings and conferences, and helped him entertain the "right associates"—all with an idea toward upward mobility in the husband's company.

Even so, they found themselves in arguments about family finances, and also found themselves resentful that their husbands seemed to have entire mornings to go fishing or play golf, while they were busy catching up with the weekly household chores. They resented their husband spending several hundred dollars on hunting and camping gear, knowing that if they decided to spend an equal amount on their dreams, there would not only be a serious argument behind closed doors, but they would then be a thousand dollars in the hole, not just five hundred.

No, nyet, nada. NONE of that was what I wanted!

I had studied enough psychology in getting my teaching credentials to know that money is one area in life about which most of us do not think rationally. We tend to be governed far more by our "feelings about money" than by math. Factors such as fear, desire, jealousy, and guilt tend to rule our purchasing choices more than "need." I did not want to be held captive by my own emotions related to money, and I did not want to be ignorant about what it might mean to have a business of my own and chart a financial destiny of my own design.

I eventually came to a point in my thinking and dreaming to determine very specific things that I personally needed for a business to BE if it was going to be for ME.

The Business Opportunity that Captured My Attention

There were three main things that were "musts" for me. You may have other "musts"—but these were my top three traits that a business had to offer if it was going to become MY business.

1. *A Realistic Opportunity.* First, I wasn't seeking to make a vast fortune. I had heard about an opportunity that held out the potential for me to earn $300 a month by working only two or three evenings a week. That seemed doable to me. It was exactly the amount I had determined I needed beyond my current salary. I was willing to take the risk of my time, and the business required only a minimal investment in products that I felt sure I could either sell or use.

The business opportunity included the potential to build a "team"—giving information and encouragement to those who might also want to grow their own business. As a trained teacher, I had confidence I could "train" others. With a great deal of experience in directing music students, I also knew something about encouragement and motivation. I had developed more than a few problem-solving skills in my time as a teacher, choir leader, and events promoter.

I did not have any hope, or desire, to recruit others in my current work environment (the college) to my business opportunity. I knew that most of my colleagues were happy with their lot in life and might even be critical of my desire for a better life for my family. I knew that my potential for "recruiting" was from a fairly large pool of people who, like me, were tired of being in a financial rut and who had bigger dreams for their lives. I felt there was a realistic opportunity for me to find those people, even though I couldn't name more than ten potential people on the day I started.

2. *A Proven Business Entity.* Second, I wasn't planning to start a business in an area where I might have to reinvent the wheel. I wanted to be associated with a broader group of similar businesses that were engaged in offering proven products and services. I wanted to be aligned with a business that had a good track record and a history of profitability. I was in a start-up mode but I didn't want any parent company I chose to be in a start-up position.

3. *An Opportunity to Work Part-Time.* Third, I wasn't planning to quit my current job in order to start my business. My business was going to be "on the side." I knew it would involve my becoming an expert in time management and that I might be working harder *initially*, but my hope was that as I learned the ropes of my new business, certain routines could be established and the trade-off would be that I would have enough money to hire some of my other responsibilities and chores done, and use the rest of the earnings to take my children on a nice

vacation, or go out to dinner occasionally and maybe even take in a play or a concert.

At the same time, I wanted to be part of a business opportunity in which there was no ceiling. I wanted to be able to grow my business as big as possible, and that meant, of course, that there would be a *potential* for the business to become full-time. I had few concerns about how long that might take. Again, at the outset, I was happy for a part-time business that could produce $300 a month!

SURELY …

SURELY …

SURELY …

I concluded there MUST be a realistic opportunity that could be profitable and part-time. I went on a quest to find that position. And I did.

My Approach to Risk

I wasn't blind to the concept of risk. Rather, I took a head-on approach to it.

I did what I have since done on a number of occasions in situations where there seemed to be "risk." I got out a blank sheet of paper, divided it into two columns, and labeled those columns:

- "What's the worst that can happen if I do this?"
- "What's the worst that can happen if I *don't* do this?"

Rather than try to overcome the anxiety associated with risk by focusing on all the *good* things that *might* be accomplished, earned, or completed, choose to take the risk HEAD ON. Explore the worst possible scenario.

After you have completed your list, turn the sheet of paper over and again, make two columns, labeling the columns:

- "What is life going to be like if I don't try?"
- "What might life be like if I do try?"

Meet Ingrid

I remember a wonderful day when my friend Ingrid and I met in Paris to do a little shopping and sightseeing. Ingrid had been a certified financial planner before she joined the same business I had joined. We met through mutual friends and found that we had many similar interests and goals. She had been in Germany conducting seminars on networking, and I had been doing the same in Poland. She took the bullet train to meet me and before we set out to explore the city, we enjoyed lunch in a lovely little café with a view.

I looked around and noted that all of the people in that little café at that hour were women. The truth everywhere seems to be that women love to shop, take time for coffee and tea, and *talk*.

We began to reminisce about the last couple of years in our mutual business. We had come into the organization at a time when it was expanding its product line greatly—but the products were displayed in print catalogs and customer orders were usually taken by phone. And then the Internet capabilities were explored and exploited and our business changed overnight! Suddenly customers could see items online, explore their options to their hearts' content, and with a couple of "clicks," an item could be in their shopping cart and by the next day, shipped out of a central warehouse on its way to their doorstep. It was like a dream come true. "Forever" had suddenly become "today."

Keep in mind always that the risks and challenges of today may very well be the rewards and opportunities of tomorrow!

In making the lists described above …

The second column on the back side of your list is where you can let your dreams find expression! You'll likely find that the first column has entries that speak to status quo, safety, security, and even tedium and boredom (if you are really honest). The second column is going to be alive with fun, adventure, and good deeds—including things yet unseen and unknown!

And *then*, decide.

- How MUCH of a risk is worth taking?
- For how long?
- With what at stake?
- With whose help?

You may find benefit in consulting with a person who has some experience with the venture you are considering. Seek out someone who has been *successful* over time (that person is likely to have had a few "downturns" along the way, and yet hasn't been overwhelmed by them). Seek out someone who genuinely wants what is best for *you*—not what they perceive could work to their advantage. Seek out a person who can be something of an accountability partner for you—someone to whom you can "report in" periodically for added counsel.

Mentors such as these are difficult to find, but they do exist. Make it a priority to find one and, in turn, be a good "mentoree." Stay accountable. Stay appreciative. Keep listening (more than you talk). You will likely find that mentors can become good friends, even if decades separate you in age.

Sharon Meers, a Silicon Valley executive and co-author of *Getting to 50/50*, recommends that a person take time to "court" a possible mentor before deciding if the relationship is a good match. She has written, "It's like picking a great professor or a great coach: Who do you respect and do they have the ability to communicate their knowledge to you in a way that you can absorb? Will they be candid with you?"

Meet Florence

Florence has been a wonderful friend and mentor to me since 1990. She and her late husband Fred were very dear to me in the most difficult time of my life.

Florence was born in Haverhill, Massachusetts, and her family lived above a little neighborhood corner store that her parents ran. Her main goal in childhood was to make some money and move away! Her father encouraged her to go to college but her mother advised her to get good grades and become an office secretary. She worked hard in school and received a scholarship to the University of Massachusetts, where she earned a degree in English and later obtained a certificate in Speech, and she taught both subjects at the high school level.

Florence told me, "In those days a girl needed a good job, a good education, and a wealthy man." She added, "And a smart girl will always have a back-up plan."

She met Fred at a summer camp where she was a counselor for girls. She knew nothing about his family but they began to correspond long distance after the summer ended. When he invited her to come to his family home, she arrived to find that he lived in a mansion, in which everything was done very properly and beautifully. The table was set with fine linens and china and a maid served the meal. For Florence, being in love with a man was not the top priority for her when it came to marriage—marrying a man with ambition was what really mattered. She chose Fred!

During the first several years, things went well. She gave birth to two beautiful daughters, but then she gave birth to a baby boy who had birth defects. He died when he was six months old. Both Florence and Fred were devastated. The doctor said such a defect wouldn't happen again, but she gave birth to another baby boy who died of the same defect. They later adopted a baby boy. All in all, it was a time of great struggle and trial.

They moved to California where Fred headed up a large food service for a non-profit group. Florence began to speak to neighborhood groups and churches—given her training and personality, she was a very popular speaker. Then, she discovered a book on different personality types and learned that she and Fred were very *different*.

As they learned how to improve their marriage, they eventually saw a need for many couples to have this information and they left their previous roles and began to have a shared speaking and writing ministry. Florence said, "I spoke for more than ten years for free before anybody ever paid me for anything I did!"

Florence is a tremendous example to me of a woman who came out of sorrow and difficulties to make a great difference in the world. Millions of people in many nations have read her books (translated into many languages) or have heard her speak.

If you can find a mentor like Florence, don't let her go! I certainly haven't.

Adventure for Its Own Sake

While I advocate that a person "weigh" risk, I am not at all adverse to the idea that sometimes "risk" can be an adventure in and of itself!

I learned to surf, long after my teenage years. There was risk, yes, but I also had a passion to "try" and that outweighed risk. I loved surfing. I survived.

I have a friend who embarked on a business venture very different than the path I have pursued. She has had some financial setbacks along the way but she is quick to say, "I wouldn't change one thing about my 'career' ups and downs. The failures were never overwhelming and periods of failure never lasted long. I learned as much or more from my failures as I did from my successes. I met interesting people and explored interesting topics in times of failure. I never had to compromise my beliefs, values, or morals. So in many ways, 'failure' was limited to money, and money can nearly always be regained. The failures made me more appreciative of success, and in the end, failures made me less uncomfortable with the idea of risk. There's risk in walking out my front door, especially on an icy morning. There's risk anytime I pull out onto a freeway. There's risk anytime I get on an airplane. But am I going to stay indoors, and never drive or fly again? Surely not!"

And by the way, she has achieved enormous financial and career success at the end of her thirty years of "ups and downs"!

There are two great quotes I recently discovered that speak to this issue of "adventure for adventure's sake." I hope they inspire you!

- *"Adventure is worthwhile in itself."* –Amelia Earhart (1897–1937).
  A pioneering American aviator, Earhart was the first person to fly

solo across the Pacific from Honolulu to California. I doubt she would have attempted, or accomplished, half of what she did if she had had any other attitude.

• *"It is better to be a lion for a day than a sheep all your life."*—Sister Elizabeth Kenny (1880–1952). She was an Australian bush nurse and pioneer in the treatment of polio.

Sheep or lion? I hope you can guess by now which I advocate!

Four Questions NOT to Ask

Finally, there are four major questions that I never encourage a person to ask. The reason? They are nearly always answered in a half-baked way, and rarely with the resounding YES they warrant. People think these questions fall into the category of "realistic" evaluation, but in truth, they don't.

1. *Do you have the time?* Well, of course you do! You have just as much time as any other person, and you will never find "more" time. The key is not in adding time, but in restructuring your present time.

In starting a new business, some things are going to move up the priority scale, other things are going to become of lesser concern to you—perhaps not forever, but for the near future. You *will* need to consider how *much* time you can allot to the start of a business. It may not be a *lot* of time, but much can be done with even *some* time. Always keep in mind that *nobody* controls your time but you.

2. *Do you have a reason for needing or wanting more money?* Of course you do! Everybody has *something* they want to do or accomplish. It may be a personal dream, a dream related to your children or grandchildren, or a cause that is near and dear to your heart.

Stop to think about what you would *really* like to do for others. Think about the legacy you want to leave behind, or the impact you want to make for the overall good of a particular person, group, or even nation.

If you don't have a need for more money, you aren't thinking very far beyond yourself.

3. *Do you have any skills that can be put to good use in a business of your own?* Of course you do!

You didn't get to adulthood without acquiring some skills and abilities. You may not have maxed out your talents yet, but you do have talents—you know it intuitively even if you have no ready evidence! Yes, you have what it takes to start a business—it is mostly a matter of *want-to* coupled with a purposed-filled dream.

If you are reading this book, I have no doubt you have the intelligence needed to learn *how* to operate a good business. Seek out a business opportunity that offers lots of training materials and helpful mentoring. You *can* succeed!

4. *Do you know people you might recruit to work with you, or who might refer you to people who will be good colleagues, customers, or associates?* Of course you do!

The key question I found myself asking was, "Do I know anyone who might like an opportunity to earn a few hundred dollars extra income in a month?" Of course I did! I began to ask other people that question, "Do *you* know anyone who might like an opportunity to earn a few hundred dollars extra income in a month?" Nearly everybody I asked knew someone! And, as soon as I had done a few small-group presentations of a business plan for the company I chose as my new business, those who had attended began asking that question to their circle of acquaintances—and even strangers—and the number of meetings grew.

In many instances, the growth of a business is primarily a numbers game. Show your business opportunity to enough people and you'll have enough customers and training recruits, and both will be connected to increased income.

Don't be afraid to ask others to a business presentation. You will be doing them a *favor*.

CHAPTER 3

The Upward Push

*BOOTSTRAPPING:
AN ENTREPRENEUR
STARTING A COMPANY
WITH VERY LITTLE CAPITAL

"Don't assume a door is closed; push on it.

Do not assume if it was closed yesterday

that it is closed today."

Marian Wright Edelman (1939–)
American Activist for Rights of Children

There are times when you think it is going to take "forever" before your business gains traction or your good idea begins to produce fruit. Hang in there! It probably *won't* take forever, and the good results may be just around the corner.

You may not be in the loop to know *all* that is just about to appear in your world—new products, new services, new methodologies.

You do not know who will be attending your sales or marketing presentation three appointments from now. There may be a go-getter who is just as eager to meet you as you are to meet her—and your business may very well expand "suddenly" in a way that you presently cannot imagine.

Don't despair at how slow the wheels seem to turn or how slowly your business seems to be growing. Keep planting good seeds and eventually a harvest *will* come.

Meet Diane

Diane is one of the most successful businesswomen I know. She also had one of the most difficult starts in life that I have ever encountered—I doubt if very many people who knew her as a child would have thought her destined for the tremendous success she has achieved. Consider her a source of inspiration as well as information!

Diane was a "downwind" baby—living downwind and downriver from a nuclear site. She was born with a birth defect that prevented her from walking until she was five years old. She had a number of medical issues early on and was taken away twice from her parents owing to their abuse. The last of these occurrences happened when she was about fifteen months old. Her mother had stabbed her in the chest, and she still has the scar to show for it. Diane lived with her grandparents for most of her childhood until their death, then went back to her parents' home, but was kicked out of the house when she was seventeen years old and has had very little contact with them since.

Diane's parents did not help her go to college, even though they were wealthy. Diane carefully engineered her own study program in college and did an internship with a CPA firm so that she could get her CPA certificate as soon as possible after she graduated. The internship meant two years of long hours with no extra pay and a very low base salary, but Diane saw it as a first job, not a last job, and certainly not a dead-end job. She managed to graduate on time, and debt free—no small feat!

Along the way, she also worked as a secretary, a bookkeeper, a computer tech, and even at one time ran ore samples from drillers in eastern Nevada. As a young CPA she worked for a large regional firm, then a smaller CPA firm, then a few years as Chief Financial Officer for a planned community under development, and then she started her own business. She's been in business for herself for twenty-five years now, has about a dozen websites that sell products to help business owners and investors, and has something of a "virtual tax firm" with CPAs across the nation.

Diane has told me on more than one occasion that she considers that she has the best job in the world because she gets to help people in many areas of business to transform their passion and purpose into real financial success. She has met with members of Congress and the Senate Finance

Committee, and been invited to special round table meetings at the White House.

She has traveled the world talking to people about business and *why* it works.

When I asked Diane to give me her top tips for a woman considering a business of her own, she said, "My goal has always been to be free. I wanted the choice to live where I wanted and how I wanted. I wanted to do work that was meaningful and to make a positive difference in the lives of others. Those have been powerful motivators."

Her specific tips!

Diane's Top 10

1. Never settle for less than you are worth.
2. Be brave. Be strong.
3. Seek out people who will lift you up and encourage you on a path of success and goodness.
4. Remember that you are a child of God.
5. Understand that your business will be a reflection of who you are—it will reflect your weaknesses and your strengths.
6. Don't try to make things too easy for others—in the end, it hurts them.
7. Don't try to "fix" people. That will hurt them, hurt you, and hurt others around you.
8. Don't let your pursuit of success keep you from being "too busy" for personal things and a family life.
9. Realize that you can never turn off your value system and ethics, so don't try.
10. Look inward and see that there is a purpose for everything you do.

Diane went from NOTHING to the top of her field. She kept building on her strengths—being good at numbers and developing strategic solutions—and she never stopped building on her strengths. The way UPWARD is always a PUSH, but it is an effective push if you are working from your strengths.

Expect to Look Back One Day and Smile!

I am thoroughly convinced that if you will give your best efforts to the business of your choice—the best of your talents, creativity, energy, and will power—you can and *will* succeed. You will one day come to the place where you can look back … and *SMILE!*

You will remember a number of special moments. They may be different from my moments, or they may be similar.

I still enjoy very simple things that are commonplace, but which I once thought of as luxuries. I don't want to ever lose appreciation for all of the little amenities and nice touches that some people seem to take for granted. I still want to feel deep gratitude in my heart, and to thoroughly *enjoy* all that I have been privileged to experience in life.

Do you remember when little bars of free soap in motel rooms were a treat? Along with the little bottles of shampoo and conditioner?

Do you remember the first time you ordered room service for breakfast and it arrived with a little vase of flowers on the tray?

Do you remember how special you felt when men wearing white gloves opened the door of the downtown *luxury* hotel for you?

Do you remember the first time you stayed in a place that HAD stars, rather than sleeping out in your car under the stars?

I do. And I'm glad the good times still far outweigh the bad.

I knew what it meant to sleep in a gas station parking lot in a "camper," and take a sponge-bath "shower" in the bathroom off the lobby of a Motel 6. But hey—I always found a way to stay clean and presentable, and to get a good night's sleep!

Pushing Yourself Forward!

There's a sign on the door of opportunity.

It says PUSH.

You are the one who is going to have to push open any door you want to walk through.

What does it mean to "push"?

It doesn't mean that you have to have a "pushy" attitude, or throw your weight around and stomp your feet in a tantrum. Far from it!

In the context of opportunity, PUSH means pushing *yourself* in ways you have not pushed yourself before.

Most of the time, when you go into business for yourself, you will quickly discover that it doesn't matter how old or young you are, how fat or thin you are, how short or tall you are, what color you are, how much formal education you have completed or not completed, or what kind of car you drive or neighborhood you live in.

Only two things matter:

- A deep desire to win

- The integrity to do your business with honesty, which is another way of saying handling money correctly.

Many people in a corporate position get to a point where they conclude they are in an unending power struggle. Their boss has the power and they have the struggle. If you are working for yourself, you may still struggle, but at least you'll have the power to control that struggle and make it do *your* bidding!

Never delude yourself. Anything worth achieving is going to take struggle.

Expect to Set New Goals as You Look at the World from the "Top"

I met the woman I just told you about, Diane, at a convention. She had been seated next to me. She was at the meeting to support her friend, Sharon Lechter, who had just written a powerful and inspiring book titled *Rich Dad, Poor Dad* with Robert Kiyosaki. Diane lived in Reno and I lived at Lake Tahoe at the time. We began to meet for lunch or coffee periodically and the more she got to know me, the more she realized that "benevolence" is a very big deal to me.

Diane asked me to come to Maui, Hawaii, the following year to speak to her business group about charity. I did that for several years. Every December I went there for ten days and spent time with the ambitious entrepreneurs who went to consult with Diane. I told them about various projects in India and Africa and showed them videos of my work with an organization called World Vision. Often when we turned the lights back on after a video presentation, I saw that many of the people there were crying. They had never thought about making money to give money away.

These entrepreneurs began to set aside money as a group to donate to charities that I represented, and along the way, a number of them began to present projects *they* had researched. At the end of the ten-day seminar they voted how their donated money should be "designated."

When I went with a group of these entrepreneurs to Rwanda, they took their own initiative in researching projects. A group of women on the team visited a coffee company run by widows of the genocide. Another man bought several properties to rent out. For my part, I focused on a charity project called "Village of Hope." It was started by two scientists who had developed a program to raise geraniums and extract the essential oils for use in spas. These scientists made agreements with the widows in the area that if they would work with them, the scientists would not only pay them good wages, but would build each of them a house that they could own completely after five years of work. I interviewed some of these women and visited the homes that they were "buying" through their labor. We were able to donate enough to build ten more homes, each with a water supply on its roof.

What a thrill it was to see these women dance around as I presented to them a solar-operated device with a New Testament in the Kinyarwandan language!

Who could ever have imagined that a solar-powered device could hold a valuable message in the Kinyarwandan language! Or that real-estate investors from a conference in Maui would contribute to its circulation!

The push to the top can mean getting to a place where you truly can be a force for good far beyond your present horizons!

The Attitudes I *Intentionally* Adopted

I made five major decisions "in my heart" during the first months and years of my pursuing a business of my own. I didn't announce them, but I wrote them down and put them where I could see them often. These were commitments concerning the ATTITUDES I chose to have.

Many people don't seem to think they can choose attitude, or see little value in doing so. Let me assure you, you can and *must* choose the prevailing attitudes you will hold consistently, no matter the circumstances or context of your life. Your attitude truly *will* determine a great deal! As the popular saying goes, "Attitude determines altitude."

I was determined *not* to adopt an attitude that contradicted, negated, or dismissed the importance of these five attitudes:

Attitude #1: Stay Teachable. I was a teacher so I knew a lot about teaching, but I also knew about *learning*. I knew I had a lot to LEARN about a business of my own.

A woman once told me, "When I first began to explore seriously the idea for having a business of my own, I had been reading a book every night by my bedside. It was a sad book that brought tears to my eyes on many nights. It was my CHECKBOOK … with very little in it."

After hearing me speak about a new business opportunity, she said, "I heard the strains of a song with a positive melody and lyrics that I could enjoy greater success in my life. I immediately responded: I want to *learn that song*!"

Learning includes WHAT TO DO, and WHAT NOT TO DO. Harriet Hall once said, "Learn from the mistakes of others. There is not enough time to make all the mistakes ourselves."

There will *always* be something you can learn that can help you do better, and be better. There will *always* be someone who knows things you don't know, and can benefit from knowing. There will *always* be more to learn about your business, your customers, your colleagues, and the opportunities that are "out there, somewhere."

Attitude #2: Be Happy. Long before people began to say routinely, "Don't worry, Be happy!" I decided I was going to be a happy person. *Joyful* may be a more accurate word. I was going to have a wellspring of joy about life deep within me that no circumstance or situation was going to quench.

Years ago I read a book that said, among many other fine things, "A person can be right or be happy." I had to think about that for a while, but I finally came to the conclusion that I agreed with the author. Some people are so intent on being *right* about an issue, they make themselves miserable in the trying, and even more miserable is the person they are trying to convince! That is often true in a marriage, and sadly, it is also common in business dealings.

The greater truth is that most things aren't worthy of the time or fight it takes to "win a point" or "get your way." It is usually far better to go on down the road, and take steps to remove the underlying causes of the trouble or find a way around them.

Attitude #3: Choose to Be a Servant. Many people are far more interested in being served than in serving. But serving is the true pathway to a life of real and lasting significance.

What matters is not the duration of your life, but the DONATION of it—the spending or giving of it as a poured-out love offering to people in need ... not just material need, but emotional and spiritual need, too.

For years, we have referred to people in government jobs as "civil servants." Sadly, there are a lot of "civil servants" who appear to have lost the meaning for both words: civil, and servant.

I have seen major leaders in many areas of our life in America fight over the smallest issues. I want to shout at times, "The fight isn't worth the effort or money! Get to a solution, swallow your pride, and do what you are in a position to do: do GOOD."

Doing good for others—without their asking you to do good, and in many cases, without their expecting you to do good—is having the attitude of a SERVANT.

Attitude #4: Give My Best and BE My Best. Everybody deserves your best effort. And your most positive attitude.

Nobody deserves *your* bad day.

Giving my best wasn't always going to translate into giving what I believed was considered BEST by another person.

I have discovered that many people need to *feel* something related to their potential for success before they can carefully and rationally hear the details of a business plan. That's quite understandable. Emotions always come before rational thought—we respond instinctively and intuitively to life, and then, if we are wise, we sit back and analyze at least a little bit what we are feeling.

This translates into practical action when we give a person a genuine compliment, or voice a word of praise or thanks. Giving our best to another person means seeing *their* best, and commenting on it—

to the person, and to others who know them (even if they are not present to hear your words).

Giving your best means voicing encouragement and an upbeat response to what *might* be, what *can* be, and what you are willing to *help* with.

Don't expect people to rise to your level before you reach out to them. Reach out to them where they are. Show them where they *can* go. And then walk with them into that new realm of existence and accomplishment.

Attitude #5: Forgive Freely. There will always be a time—or many times—when another person disappoints you in some way. Choose to forgive. And, to forgive quickly and freely.

Unforgiveness is like deciding to medicate your pain by drinking a poison and expecting the *other* person to die. The person who has hurt you may not care in the least that you forgive, or don't forgive. Your harboring unforgiveness may not impact that hurtful person in the least. In fact, the hurtful person may never even realize you have been wounded, or care that you have been. YOU are the one who needs to forgive in order to set yourself free.

Creating a *Family* Business

The way you push yourself is going to be "felt" by others in your family. The best approach is not to *push* others, but rather, to encourage your children to join with you in a quest for greater excellence. Find creative ways to encourage them to push themselves to gain "more" out of life!

When they were really quite young, I "paid" my children for selling some of the products I sold. They took these products door to door in various neighborhoods in the city where we lived, and they learned to sell with enthusiasm and eagerness. They had all the answers about what the products could do to enhance a person's life, how to use the products, and *why* their products made more sense than similar products in the local supermarket or drugstore. I think there were many days when they saw this as a game—a competitive challenge that had real "winnings" associated with it. They had fun with selling. And they did well!

If they chose not to sell on a given day, they forfeited the potential rewards associated with selling. They were not punished. They simply didn't receive the benefits.

As a family:

• *We set goals together.* I told my children when I reached a certain dollar amount in sales they would both be rewarded.

• *My children frequently went along on my one-on-one business appointments.* If I made an appointment at a family-friendly restaurant, I scheduled the appointment at a time when the restaurant wasn't likely to be very busy. I got a table for the children several tables away from me and my prospective client. I gave the children homework to do, or crayons and coloring books, told the waitress that I would give her a big tip at the end of our stay, and also let my children know that I was not to be interrupted, they were to work quietly, and that if they did a good job of both, an ice cream cone just might be in their future.

• *I often took the children with me to seminars and conferences out of town.* I would arrange for a baby sitter during the conference sessions, but the rest of the time, I made our trip an adventure. We had "car picnics" and on many occasions, we slept in our car. After the final session of the conference, I took them to the local zoo or a park, which was a fun activity for them.

• *I instilled in my children that our business was just that—OUR family business.* I included them in the putting together of orders and going with me to deliver them—back in the days before computerized ordering and delivery. I taught them how to use the products I sold so they could help me with home chores.

• *I made sure my children were well cared for any time I had to be out of the house on a business presentation or appointment to which they could not go.* I took a page out of my mother's book and bartered or exchanged "babysitting" services with a trusted older friend my children enjoyed being with. I made sure my children's meals were provided and that their homework was done. I did not leave their welfare to chance—I made sure at all times that they were my top priority. After all, *they* were the number-one reason I wanted additional income.

Meet Martina

I first met Martina in Eugene, Oregon, where I was performing in the choir at the Oregon Bach Festival. Helmuth Rilling was the conductor and artistic director of the festival, and Martina is his wife. At the time we first met, she had just arrived from Germany with her two little girls. I highly admired the balancing act she was doing, keeping up with her husband's busy concert schedule, performing herself on the flute and singing in the choir, caring for the two children, and managing their schedule around the world.

Martina was born during World War II to a Jewish family in Leipzig. She was hidden until the war was over. The family then fled to West Germany when the communist regime came in. Later, she was able to study flute in Italy and then she met Helmuth who was conducting all over Europe. After they married they came to New York where Helmuth studied with Leonard Bernstein while Martina studied flute with Julius Baker, first flutist of the New York Philharmonic.

Through the years I watched Martina as we traveled together to many places. Always, she was the consummate balancer of family care, the keeper of her husband's schedule, and the gracious greeter and hostess for the many music patrons they met along the way. She also sang in countless performances in his professional choir, Gaechinger Kantorei.

She was responsible for the care of their properties, the Bach Academy, and the finances of their family and Helmuth's professional obligations. With Helmuth, she carefully watched over their daughters' musical training—Sara on the viola and Rahel on the violin. Both young women are now very accomplished and have professional careers of their own. Rahel is married to David Adorjan, a professional cellist. They now have a beautiful young son named Joseph, who at two years old is already very musical. Sara is married to Carsten Kretschmann, a professor at Stuttgart University and an accomplished pianist.

Martina has raised a significant family and given great contributions of herself to thousands upon thousands of people. I count her a very dear friend and am so proud of all she has done.

Rarely do you find such a family as this working "in synergy" as they have combined their talents, personalities, and business skills to bring profound inspiration to many nations. I am honored to be a friend to each person in the Rilling family. They are one of the finest examples I know of a "family business."

The One Thing You Must Never Doubt

There is one thing you must never doubt once you have made a firm commitment to push yourself forward in a business of your own. You must never doubt the validity of your DREAM!

Every person has dreams. Some of them may have been dormant for a long time. Some dreams may be recently conceived, others from childhood. Some dreams may be too fantastic to ever enter reality. But many, many dreams are ones that *can* be translated into goals and plans, and therefore, can be achieved. Those are the dreams worth pursuing with a great deal of focus and energy. Those are the dreams that really can come true!

Through the years, I have asked a number of audiences in a variety of venues to tell me their dreams—spontaneously calling them out to me from their seats. I've heard …

- Freedom
- Travel
- More hope
- More time for doing what I enjoy most
- Better options and choices
- Security
- Fishing
- Tuesdays at home alone with my own thoughts
- Time with my spouse
- Sleep—lots of sleep
- Sleeping in on a Monday morning!

What is it that you dream of doing just for the *fun* of it? What do you dream about having *more* of? What do you dream of accomplishing in your lifetime, and leaving behind as a legacy? What do you dream of seeing, of saying, of experiencing?

Every person has a dream. I believe we each are born with an innate, lingering desire to do something, be something, and have something in this life. We have an innate desire to produce something that lasts beyond our lifetime—for our benefit in eternity, and for the benefit of others left behind on this earth. Dreaming is part of our design, our makeup as human beings.

The best dreamers are not the ones who dream while they are asleep, and not even those who can remember their night dreams when they awaken. The best dreamers are those who dream with their eyes wide open and refuse to quit pursuing their dreams until their dreams are a reality.

Staffan Olson in India was a person with this kind of dream. He saw precious children living in beggars' poverty on the streets who needed love and care. He worked tirelessly for those children to be brought in off the streets, to be fed, to live in a clean place and sleep in a safe environment, and to be dressed in crisp well-made uniforms. Today, that's a reality!

It didn't happen in Staffan's corner of the world, however, before Staffan dreamed the dream and worked to make it happen.

I have met some amazing dreamers in my life. Some of them have been quite young at the time of our meeting. Others have been quite elderly. I assure you of this: These dreamers inspired me more than I could ever inspire them!

- One sixteen-year-old girl told me her dream is to be a headmaster of a school that has "entrepreneurial skills" as part of the curriculum.

- A woman at the age of 101 told me she delivers "meals on wheels" to *old people*, and dreams of doing it for years to come.

The lesson to draw: Dreamers come in all ages and pursue all types of dreams—the vast majority of which are good, for both themselves and others.

A dreamer has a dream.

But eventually …

A dream *makes* a dreamer.

The Advantage of Having Wise Counselors

Dreams also must be backed up with wise counsel. A truly wise counselor will never try to squelch your dream—rather, a wise counselor will give you practical advice about how to achieve your dream in a way that is legal, makes good business sense, and is beneficial to everybody involved.

Meet Clarissa

My beautiful friend Clarissa had a goal as a young girl to be a fashion model and work for Sears catalogue. She had no idea she would go far beyond that in her modeling career. As a young woman, she became a famous superstar model in Europe where she produced many television shows having to do with beauty, one being the Miss Universe pageant. She was on more than 250 covers of fashion magazines.

In spite of little encouragement from her family she kept moving ahead to her ultimate dream, which was to have *a business of her own.* Her advice to women who are thinking about starting a business is this: "Before going into any business venture, have a good lawyer look at anything you need to sign beforehand. I learned the hard way that a lawyer must review all legal documents. Either way, the lawyer is going to be paid."

Never forget that lawyers are often called by the term "counselor"!

As you gain wise counsel, there are two types of "counselors" that you need to ignore:

1. *Don't Listen to the Accusers.* Don't let anybody ever accuse you of being greedy or materialistic because you want more money and are willing to work hard to earn it. Nobody but you knows *why* you want a

better life for yourself and others. And therefore, nobody but you can fully understand your own motives or the ways in which more money may help you fulfill personal dreams.

My friend Jeanette told me that the reason she wanted to earn more money was so she could pay her beloved grandmother's monthly bills. She didn't want her grandmother to be worried about finances in her last years. She said, "Granny, I am going to give you some large envelopes that are prestamped. Every month when the bills come for your utilities and other expenses, don't even open those bills. You put them in one of those envelopes and send it to me and I'll take care of the bills." And Granny did what she was told to do, and my friend did what she had promised to do. How wonderful is that? It is far from any definition I hold for materialistic or greedy.

2. *Don't Listen to the Naysayers.* Don't listen to those who tell you that you can *never* fulfill your dream. Don't waste time or energy conversing or arguing with them. Simply go out and prove them wrong!

Rekindle and Revisit Your Dreams

Kindle and rekindle your own dreams.   Revisit them often. There are three great advantages to doing this:

Advantage #1: Encouragement of Self. It is a great thing to be motivated or encouraged by others. It is even greater to tap into your own ability to encourage yourself.

Every person has moments of self-doubt about whether they truly can reach their goals or succeed in grasping their dreams. When those moments come, seek out words of encouragement spoken by others.

Consider the encouragement below. Nelson Mandela had a good perspective on human value. He said this in his 1994 inaugural speech:

> Our deepest fear is not that we are inadequate. Our deepest fear is that we are powerful beyond measure. It is our light, not our darkness, that most frightens us. We ask ourselves, who am I to be brilliant, gorgeous, talented, and fabulous? Actually, who are you *not* to be? You are a child of God. Your playing small doesn't serve the world. There is nothing enlightened about shrinking so that other people won't feel insecure around you. We are born to make manifest the glory of God that is within us. It's not just in

some of us, it's in everyone. And as we let our own light shine, we unconsciously give other people permission to do the same. As we are liberated from our own fear, our presence automatically liberates others. (www.bet.com/news/global/2013/12/05)

Advantage #2: You Will Have Encouragement for Others. I once was describing the fun I had at international-airport duty-free shops to an audience. I had eye contact with a woman who conveyed loud and clear with her facial expressions, "Yeah, like that could ever happen to *me*."

I felt like responding immediately, "You have put the emPHASis on the wrong word. It should be, 'Like that *could* ever happen to me.' I know—because it happened to *me*."

I didn't stop my talk to address her skepticism, but let me assure you, a better life *can* happen to YOU!

As you begin to focus on your dream and pursue it with your whole heart, your enthusiasm for your dream will become infectious. And as you begin to realize your dream and enjoy its reality, your example will motivate and encourage others.

Advantage #3: It Will Help You Keep Your Cup Right-Side Up! One night I was rushing to a meeting in southern California after returning to the United States from an overseas trip. I was quite "jet-lagged" and anxious to have the meeting behind me. I ducked backstage to find a cup of coffee to help me wake up! In the dark, I grabbed a big mug and reached for the lever on the coffee container and pulled it down—only to feel hot coffee spill onto me. I looked at the coffee on my bright red evening gown, and figured, "The damage is done. But I still need coffee!" So I tried again and this time the coffee covered even more of my dress.

I had been holding the mug upside down!

Keep your cup up—stay open to learning and doing new things, but be alert that you are truly in the right position to *receive* all that others offer to teach you!

As you draw both information and inspiration from others, your dream will take on greater definition and clarity. Your inner reservoir of motivation will become filled, and your dream will permeate your entire life.

Dreams Develop as You Grow

Expect your dream to *grow* as you begin to turn dreams into reality. Dreams expand, far more readily than they contract—but this is only true if you remain committed to your dreams and work toward their accomplishment.

During those first months after I moved to Bend, Oregon, my sister Barbara knew I missed the family and big city life so she arranged for me to speak at the Alumni Association meeting for our alma mater, Point Loma University in San Diego. I knew it was a love gift from her to allow me a little vacation from gleaning beans and picking strawberries. And I was delighted to go! It was such fun to see old college friends, and also to be back in a "city" environment.

I realized during that trip that one of the things I fully intended to do if I ever had enough money to do it, was to travel and visit with close friends and family. My dream expanded on that trip from "making more money to provide more for my children" to, "making more money to also provide more travel opportunities for us as a family"!

I believe many people have a desire to travel, they just don't have the money to spend on airfare or travel expenses. Years later, I had an inner feeling that one of my favorite uncles, whom we called Tedo, wasn't going to be with us much longer. I pulled my children out of school, bought plane tickets for us, and we went to visit Uncle Tedo for two days. He died a month later. Do you think I regretted the money spent on that trip? Not a penny's worth.

During our visit, Uncle Tedo wanted to buy a ball and bat for my son Paul, and then he insisted we go to the park. We bundled Uncle Tedo up in a blanket and let him sit on the park bench. I pitched and Paul hit the ball and Debi, my daughter, was the catcher. Uncle Tedo laughed and clapped with great enthusiasm. That trip to the park to watch his great-niece and great-nephew play ball was like a million dollars to him. And I wouldn't trade that memory for a million dollars today.

My dream also expanded in yet another dimension. My initial dreams for my business were focused on my children. I gradually allowed myself to be factored into my own dreams as I earned more and became more successful.

I began to enjoy giving experiences to *Beverly*. I discovered that I really *do* enjoy shopping—something I didn't even know I was missing when I was poor.

I personally love to shop at duty-free stores, and since I travel a great deal through airports that *have* duty-free stores, this is also a very convenient time to find unusual gifts, clothing, and items for my home. I especially enjoy the fact that most duty-free stores have a shipping department. I love to come home to find boxes awaiting me!

Through the years, I've learned to define "duty free" in a slightly different way. I now know how to have fresh flowers, specialty meats and fruits, clothing, health and beauty products, and many necessary home-care items sent to me directly. If the clothes don't fit or don't turn out to be the quality I want or a style that is as flattering as I had hoped … well, with a quick message written online, the item could be on its way back to the seller. What a way to shop! That's hassle-free shopping as far as I'm concerned … it is truly "duty free" in that I am free of the "duties" involved in the process!

What woman doesn't have a life filled with duties. Getting rid of some of those duties is nearly always a welcomed idea!

Let me give you full permission today—dream BIG dreams. Dream them for others you love. And dream them for yourself.

Dreams have a magnetic pull to them—the bigger and stronger the magnet of your dream, the easier you will find PUSHING yourself toward the success you desire.

CHAPTER 4

Purpose for Profit

*BOOTSTRAPPING:
AN ENTREPRENEUR
STARTING A COMPANY
WITH VERY LITTLE CAPITAL

"If you want a place in the sun, you've got

to put up with a few blisters."

Abigail Van Buren (Pauline Phillips) (1918–2013)
American Advice Columnist, known as "Dear Abby"

One of the most basic definitions of business is "commercial activity involving the exchange of money for goods or services." Business involves making money, and more specifically, making a *profit*. It also requires commercial activity, otherwise known as *work*.

If you make money without work you are likely winning a lottery or sweepstakes—which requires little more than the purchase of a ticket and luck. Very, very, very few people succeed at this, of course.

If you are working without making money, you may be doing volunteer service, being a full-time homemaker and parent, or you may have been conscripted as a slave of some type.

If you are exchanging goods or services for money, but you aren't making a *profit*, you aren't really in business. You are simply bartering. Profit means that you are taking in more than you are shelling out, which means that you have a margin of money to spend on things you need or want.

In sum, business means making a profit, and working to do so.

I realize that "profit" has become a dirty word in some circles, but think about it—how hard are you willing to work without profit?

A speaker once asked, "Ladies, would you rather be right or rich?"

My answer is that I want to be BOTH right AND rich. It is wealth that will allow me to set some injustices right, and to do the right things that benefit all people, and often, very specific people that God seems to have put in my direct path. While I will *not* compromise my values when it comes to what is right or wrong, I see no reason to fail in exercising good business sense, or purposefully to make myself poor in order to show that I am a person of virtue or kindness. I much prefer to be a person of virtue AND kindness who can help others in need in very practical, tangible, and material ways.

Let me assure you, even the most noble ministry efforts require *funding*. Are you aware that some of the great saints down through history spent an amazing percentage of their time in *fundraising* to secure the necessities for those they served, and for those who served alongside them?

I like the speaker who said, "The nice thing about money is that it goes with everything. It never clashes with anything I wear."

Income and Other Money Matters

I learned very quickly that if I had my own business, or was affiliated with a larger company that allowed me to function as a sole-business owner, I could earn whatever I wanted to earn. That isn't true in the corporate world as a whole.

The statistics still tell us that women earn less than men in the corporate world. In some cases women earn forty percent less for doing comparable tasks. It isn't *just*, but it is still a reality that confronts us. The statistics also tell us that women tend to put more effort into a day than men—many women have two full-time jobs. One they do outside their home for an "employer" for eight to nine hours, and another they do before and after in their work at home for another seven to eight hours, and if you add it all up, there's barely enough time for a decent night's sleep before the grind starts all over.

Working for a Salary. Let's consider for a minute what happens to a person who "works for a salary."

There are several things that apply to most salaried employees:

• *Somebody ELSE tells them what to do and when to do it—and gives the deadline by which the task must be completed.* Projects or duties are "assigned," and there rarely is any freedom to decide who is going to be on your "work team" if more than one person is required to complete a particular task or project by a particular date.

• *Somebody OTHER THAN SELF also dictates the time to show up at the workplace and what time is acceptable to leave at the end of the workday.* The salaried employee should never assume that this will be an eight-hour or nine-hour span of time.

I heard a woman say recently, "If I get to work after 7:30 in the morning, people want to know what happened to make me late … even though the official workday doesn't start until 8:00 AM. If I leave before 7:30 in the evening, I'm considered a slug—not holding up my fair share of the workload and mutual workplace stress. I'm *expected* to work sixty hours a week—if I take time away from my desk for lunch, I'm expected to make that up on Saturday. This isn't a full-time job. It's a full-time life. And it isn't a life I am choosing. It is one in which I have little to say if I want to stay employed."

• *Somebody ELSE dictates how many breaks the salaried employee can take, how many donuts she can take from the lunchroom tray and still be considered "polite," when she can take vacation days, and what she can have in the way of personal items in her office or cubicle.*

• *Somebody ELSE determines the salaried person's income, and how frequently that amount can change—and also determines her job description, and how frequently she will be evaluated on performing the duties of the job to somebody else's level of approval.*

Because somebody else is determining the salary, somebody else is also determining what type of house the salaried person can live in and what type of car she can drive. Somebody else is defining the "cultural norm" of the workplace—which ultimately will include standards about where it is acceptable for a salaried person to vacation and dine, and what types of hobbies are "appropriate" for her to pursue. To a great extent, somebody else will be dictating what she wears, including what types of jewelry and accessories she wears.

Because somebody else is determining both her salary and work demands, that somebody else is probably also determining how many children she will have, and when—after all, maternity leave is a benefit that doesn't always feel like a benefit, and somebody else likely will make it very clear *when* it is inconvenient for the salaried employee to get pregnant.

One of the key questions I ask women—in every nation where I have an opportunity to ask women—is this: "Who is defining your life?"

Culture has a role. Government has a little something to say in some nations. Spouses and family constraints are a factor in some places. But one main area in which many women have a say in the "defining" is the job that they choose to do—the work they choose to undertake, the career path they choose to develop. The question of "Who is defining your *work* life?" is a question that many women can answer, if they only will.

Meet Bev

I have met a number of women through the years who have let their childhood "environment" define them. My friend Bev is not one of them!

She grew up in rural New Mexico—miles from the nearest town—in an adobe house with no electricity, no running water, and no indoor toilet. Her house was on a dirt road, and more times than she can count, her family found itself stuck in the mud after a rainstorm.

As a girl, she walked to school, and she and her brother had the responsibility for carrying two large buckets of water to the school from a spring near their home. The buckets had originally held lard, so they had lids. This water was the school's drinking water and her family was paid seven dollars a month by the county for this "water service."

In the years when the school did not have at least eight students, all of the children were driven in a Jeep to a school twenty-two miles from her home.

When the snow was deep in winter, a nearby rancher loaned Bev and her brother a horse to ride to school. She has lots of memories of riding a black horse named Jack, with both she and her brother holding on to a bucket of water!

If Bev had let her "start in life" define her "level of achievement in life," she would never have done anything!

She refused to let any circumstance of her life define her.

Who Determines How Much You Make? I once heard a speaker ask, "What does it take for a woman to succeed in business?" I adapted that question to be, "What does it take for a woman to start her own business?"

In many cases, for many women, it takes a MAN.

But before you conclude that you *know* what I mean, read on.

There are many women who have a chauvinistic boss, and they are sick and tired of his antics.

There are other women who are tired of "playing the game" that their male boss requires for them to get a promotion.

There are still other women who are weary of getting to do all the work, getting no increase in pay, and getting no appreciation from their male supervisor.

Yes, there is a MAN at the root of her desire to build her own business!

In other cases, there is a man at home. But he isn't helping with the children. He insists that she work and earn money. And he doesn't really care what she does as long as his dinner is prepared on time, the children are cared for, and some money comes in.

In some cases, there is a man who is becoming increasingly critical and difficult to live with, and she isn't sure how long her marriage is going to last.

Yes, there is a MAN at the root of her desire to stay at home and build her own business.

Before you conclude that I am down on all men, I am not. But I do realize that there are literally millions of women around the world who are chafing right now under the iron rule of a man in the workplace, or under the emotional abuse of a man in their home.

For many of these women, a "business of their own" seems almost an impossible dream.

In truth, it is very often the most *realistic* and *best* solution for a woman who is being completely dominated by a man who does not have her best interests at heart.

I encourage you to do several things today since you likely are *not* a woman who fits this description, or may fit the description but not to a degree of dire despair.

First, read, research, "google," and otherwise inform yourself about the situation in which you are working, living, or the community environment around you.

Second, pray for wisdom that you can, and believe that you *will*, find a better way!

There is a tremendous "good" to be achieved by those who are willing to develop a business in order to employ or provide a business opportunity to women who are currently caught in the clutches of poverty, low self-value, or a dead-end financial future.

The Issue of Debt

I asked an audience one January how many present had started the new year with a hangover. I did *not* ask for a show of hands, but I could tell by the many winks and nods that I had hit a chord.

And then I said, "I believe *all* of you started the year with a very bad hangover."

Many seemed startled at that, a few registered resistance to the idea.

I quickly added, "It was the hangover of debt. And even if you didn't feel the ache of that hangover in your personal finances, you still had the hangover if you are a citizen of the United States. We are a nation that is deeply in debt, and it is every bit as debilitating as an alcohol-induced hangover in the long run of our lives, and on into the lives of our children."

In my opinion, we need to get sober, and get sober quickly.

There is a cure for the national debt, one that few politicians will address because they know it isn't something they can legislate. We need more people earning more money. This means an increase in productivity, which translates into a greater GNP for our nation. It means a rebalancing of trade agreements with nations that are ripping us off. It means a willingness to spend less and save more—both individually in our families and collectively as a nation. It means putting less on credit cards and paying cash as a "rule," not just occasionally.

These are not impossible things to do. For some, however—people I might call the debt-oholics—they are difficult things to do.

Here is an important fact you may not know: The amount of "private debt" in our nation is twice as large as the federal debt.

Years ago I made it a focused goal in my business to get out of personal debt and stay there. I calculated one day how much debt I had, against the assets I had, and concluded that if that trend continued and things were not drastically turned around in my life, I was going to be in big trouble by the time the "retirement years" rolled around. I made changes. I worked *extra hard*. And I dug myself out of debt. If I could do it, you can.

One of the things I discovered was that as soon as I made my mind up that I was going to shed debt and live debt-free, all sorts of temptations to "buy" popped up. There was the person who wanted me to buy a boat and a cabin in the woods, another person who came along with a land deal in Florida, and yet another with a "cactus" farm in Arizona. There were temptations to "just try on" the expensive fur coat or the elegant necklace.

I did not completely quit using credit cards. Rather, I *limited* my credit cards to purchases directly related to my business, and I disciplined myself to pay off those credit cards every month. This is something the credit-card companies don't really want a person to do— they only make serious money on the *interest* they can charge you. It was a convenient way for me to keep track of my business expenses, however, and I saw it as a technique for money management.

I also did not completely rid myself of mortgage debt for several years. But that payment was the only payment in my life that had an "interest" amount attached to it. And eventually, I eliminated mortgage payments in my life, too.

I advise you strongly NOT to go into debt to build your business. I took an approach that I would only invest money into the growing of my business if I could see clearly that I was going to have an increase in profits to pay for the additional investment.

I put a renewed emphasis on developing customers who were good "retail" customers for real products. As an example, if I needed money to go to a conference or a special meeting, and I needed money for babysitting in order to attend that seminar, I translated the amount I needed into "how many of a particular item do I need to sell in order to make that much money?" I continually had selling goals, not necessarily earning goals. There's a difference and it's a difference worth learning and calculating often.

It is fun for many businesses to encourage their employees to dream of exotic vacations and expensive luxury items, but if I had the choice of having those items in my life and the freedom of being debt-free, I'll take debt-free any day!

I remember vividly the day I received a statement from Texaco saying—to my surprise—"credit, do not pay." I had overpaid $25.66 on that account by mistake. I spent the next three weeks almost euphoric that if all else failed in my life, I still had a tank of gas! (I realize, of course, that this gas price was before most of you were born.)

Not long after that I came across a quote that I had sitting on my desk for years: "The man who rolls up his sleeves seldom loses his shirt."

The way out of most debt is to work harder. Harder doesn't *always* translate into greater effort or the pain of heave-ho lifting. It can mean putting in more hours. It can also mean working smarter. And, in many instances, it can mean recruiting more people to work with you so that part of what *they* are doing translates into a dividend, royalty, or percentage back to you as the one who recruited and trained them.

Work Is ESSENTIAL

You can avoid work—but you will not be successful in *business*.

Work is an equal-opportunity issue. It doesn't matter to "Work" who is putting out the effort, time, or strategizing. Work only cares that the work gets done! A good worker can be a single or married person, a single parent or a parent with a large family. It can be a person who is black, white, Asian, Hispanic, or pink with purple polka dots. Work doesn't care about a person's age or social standing or cultural background. Work says simply, "Do the work, and you will get the reward for doing it." In most cases, that reward will be tangible, and very likely, financial.

Those who don't work, don't earn. (And let's be clear on this, a welfare check from the government isn't really a *good* amount of "earning" and the amount of money is far less than what can be achieved through working—I don't care how clever a person may be in manipulating the system. If people who are smart enough to "cheat" the rest of us would put their brain power and energy into real work attached to real wages, they'd be far better off, and so would the rest of the taxpayers who are supporting them.)

When You Define Your Business, You Define Your "Work"

Let me give you several questions that you should weigh about the business opportunity you desire to pursue:

- *Are you happy with your current retirement plan? Does the business opportunity allow you the opportunity to develop a fund to pay for the lifestyle you want in your older years?*

You will be wise to set aside a portion of your earnings, even from the beginning, for a "savings account" that you don't touch, but that you allow to build with compound interest. Think long range. Part of what you will be *working* for is a good retirement later in life.

- *Do you want to sell products, or services, or both?*
- *Do you want to be in retail or wholesale?*
- *What licensing laws or regulations might impact a home business in the area where you live?*
- *What will it cost to market your product or service?*
- *What do you see as your first year's goals (for sales, net profit, visibility in the marketplace)?*
- *What do you need financially to get started? How much cash will you need in the first twelve months of your business?*

The answers to these questions will generate a framework for the nature of your work as you develop your business plan. They will tell you *how* you will need to order your workdays to meet your goals.

Getting Started. My husband Arthur tells the story of how his father, during the Great Depression, overcame a desperate situation to earn money. He walked into the main office of an insurance company and asked for a job. The manager told him they weren't hiring. He responded with an answer I regard as brilliant: "Does that mean you are selling all the insurance you want to sell?" The manager replied, "No ..."

Arthur's father then said, "If you will hire me, I will outsell every agent in your office for the next month. If I don't, you don't have to hire me permanently." The manager agreed. Needless to say, Arthur's father *did* outsell every other agent in the office, and continued to do so month after month for all the years he worked there.

Determination and commitment. They are two indispensable qualities.

The business I chose had a very low buy-in level compared to many large companies that offer small-business-owner franchises or distributorships. Furthermore, it was highly advantageous to me that I could sell product that would apply toward my purchase of *more* product.

- *What kind of help will you need in your new business, and where are you going to find that person or persons?*

The business I started had lots of routine chores connected to it— placing orders, picking up and distributing orders, keeping records, and so forth. I went to a nearby high school and asked the main business teacher to link me to the sharpest girl who was good in business—an "A" student who was conscientious and who would work for a dollar above minimum wage. I found just such a girl and this young woman helped me with a mountain of paperwork and filing!

- *What business structure will best suit your needs and the personal constraints of your life?*

I believe it is wisdom to keep your business records and your family finances separate. Keep a separate set of books. Have a checking account for your business. Designate a separate phone number for your business. That way, you can always be available to your children or other family members who will feel more secure in knowing that you can receive a call and return one quickly.

- *How much physical space will you need for your new business?*

I didn't have much space, but for the business I chose, I didn't need much space! Many home businesses only require a few square feet—perhaps a desk or work table and a place to store some file boxes.

I started out with a corner of my living room, working at my dining room table, with a couple of drawers set aside for storing portable files.

In today's world, there are countless pieces of inexpensive furniture that can do double-duty. Be creative!

- *What are your personal and financial objectives?*

Your personal and financial goals will be directly related to each other as you begin to work and make a profit. Only you can answer this key question and the answer may not translate easily to a spreadsheet.

Avoiding the "Rut" of Work. For the most part, I find women to be nearly universally creative in the way they adorn themselves and their homes, and conduct their daily chores. When I look out over a sea of people at a major convention, I never see two women dressed *exactly* alike (unless, of course, they are wearing a prescribed uniform). And even if their garments appear alike or similar, I would bet money that their undergarments are different. Plus, their makeup is different, their accessories are different, and their hairstyles are different.

Men, not so much. Suits are still suits, whether two- or three-piece. Ties and shirts are still the norm in the business world. It's high "creativity" if a guy decides he doesn't need to wear socks with his loafers, and he'd probably be wise to *be* in the fashion industry or near a beach if that's his choice.

The challenge we face in business is the challenge of being creative in our *schedules* and the choices we make from day to day.

I once saw a cartoon in which two men were riding on the subway, both of them reading a newspaper. One guy looked at the other guy and said, "I forget—are we going to work or are we coming home?"

Some days feel that way, don't they? And sadly, for some people, *most* workdays feel that way. There is a routine to be followed, and much of the future seems to be "pre-packaged." Many people can tell you exactly how many years they need to stay employed in their current job before they will be eligible for a raise ... or promotion ... or retirement. They are like students who can tell you how many months before graduation.

When I knew that I was going to be able to quit my "day job" of teaching at a college, and pursue my business full-time, I was filled with excitement. I saw it as a "graduation day" for me so I scheduled my last day of full-time "employment" at the college on *graduation day*. There were hundreds of people around me in somber robes. I had to wear a robe, too—after all, I was a professor. But I also rebelled in my own way. I wore sunglasses throughout the entire ceremony. That was strictly forbidden—but hey, what could they do to me? I was "outta there" the minute the recessional was over! I wasn't trying to look "cool," but I was taking a step toward distancing myself from my old surroundings.

I have a friend who said one day, "I've had it with dressing for success. They say you should dress for what you *want*, and I have all the success I want. I'm going to start dressing for *vacation*."

That was my attitude.

Let me ask you today, "Do you see your work as drudgery ... a rut ... a place to put in your time until your next reward? Or, do you see your work as an adventure? Does it feel more like vacation-style fun than the bondage of a factory line (even if you don't work in a factory)?"

One Christmas, I took my two children to Disneyland. We flew to Anaheim and went on Saturday before Christmas—a busy time with lots of noise and excitement. Then we went back on Christmas Day and rode all the rides three or four times—whatever the kids wanted— because there was *nobody* in the park that day. We let the children do their own Christmas shopping at Disneyland. I've rarely laughed so much in my life, or had greater pleasure in watching my children have a good time!

Another Christmas, when the children were older, I took them and some of their friends on a ski trip. We stayed at a lodge right next to the ski lift so I could sit on the deck and watch them come down the mountain, and never feel a need to put on skis or get in the car. I gave the kids the freedom to order whatever they wanted in the restaurant and charge it to their room, and I allowed them to watch television movies that we had brought with us—all night if they wanted to. It sure did *feel* like Christmas to the kids, and to me ... and there was no putting up or taking down decorations or spending hours in the kitchen cooking and cleaning up. We had the traditional Christmas feast in the lodge restaurant by a roaring fireplace, and God provided snowflakes outside the window. It was magical.

Not every year has been Disneyland or ski resort—but I think Christmas is a good time for a person to be as creative as possible, and "work" at it in the *least* possible way!

That's my choice. It is part of the luxury I enjoy in having my own business. I'm not limited to a set number of "days off" from work, and I don't have any corporate office parties I have to attend!

Finding Alternatives. There are always a number of different ways to get the same tasks, or same amount of work, *done*. I believe there is a rule from the health-care industry that could be applied to just about any profession:

DO NO HARM.

Even if you can't bring about a cure or a major improvement, you *can* do your utmost to keep from doing harm!

Taking this approach *can* greatly free many women from an overly developed sense of "obligation" or "responsibility" that slows them down and contributes little benefit to others.

Let me explain further.

I have met numerous women who tell me they don't have "time" for a part-time, at-home business. Why not? Because they are too busy taking care of a husband, children, and in some cases, a parent. When I ask these women to tell me the *specifics* of what they are doing for their loved ones, I usually come away with a sense that they are doing things that their loved ones are neither requesting nor requiring. They are doing things *they* think a good wife/mother/daughter *should* do.

Would there be any harm done in not washing, starching, and ironing their husband's shirts when a good laundry just a block away will do them to perfection at a very reasonable price—and especially so if the family budget allows for the processing of five such shirts a week?

Would they be doing any harm by encouraging their children to go out and make up their own play several afternoons a week after school, rather than enrolling their child in lessons or activities five days a week at a considerable expense for lessons, dues or fees, uniforms, sporting gear or project supplies, and lots of chauffeuring time? Would their children perhaps *enjoy* a little more free time just to read, work on a craft or art project, or engage in make-believe play with various toys or games that are relatively inexpensive or that can be created by the children themselves?

Would there be any harm in not polishing every piece of furniture every day? Any harm in insisting that the children (or spouse) help clear the table after dinner and put the dishes in the dishwasher? Any harm in requiring a child to help set the table for dinner, stir the gravy, empty the trash, or feed the dog?

Would there be any harm in insisting that a spouse NOT throw his discarded clothing on the floor, and instead put it into a designated laundry basket? Would there be any harm in insisting that an elderly parent keep a log of medications taken daily, and perhaps keep that log on a form that can be computerized and be available online?

Where is it written that a *woman* needs to do chores or take on responsibilities that are not gender-specific? And in truth, most daily practical chores are *not* gender-specific. Men *can* learn to run a vacuum cleaner or do a load of laundry or keep sidewalks swept.

I can hardly tell you how "liberated" from chores I felt on the day when I realized that I *could* take my children out of school for a two-week travel experience to another continent—and hire a tutor to help them catch up on any course content they had missed.

I was just as "liberated" from chores the day I realized that I had enough money to have my house cleaned once a week, and later, when I was able to hire a cook to prepare the meals I wanted to eat.

Ask yourself about every area of your life—especially your "must do" chores and any responsibilities that you believe require you to be in charge: What is truly *required*? Required by whom? And if something is required, why do *you* need to be the one doing what is required?

Ask, is there an alternate way of getting something done and "do no harm" in the process?

Ask yourself, why do I feel *obligated* to do some things—is it something I was told as a child, or something that someone is requiring of me because of what *they* were told as a child?

Ask, what *might* you do with the time you are currently spending in chores that need to be done again almost as soon as you complete the "required" task? Could you perhaps enjoy tea or coffee in a little café with a view? Could you perhaps take in the smell of fresh salt air from a beach-front cottage? Could you perhaps enjoy watching your children laugh hilariously as they ride in a horse-drawn sleigh over snow fields in a high mountain area? Could you take in the sights of Munich or Oslo or New Delhi?

"Yeah, right," a woman said after hearing me ask these questions. "Like I could do that."

I replied, "Well, you *could*, if you are willing to work for it!"

Don't Waste Your Time. Work is technically defined as an amount of "task" completed in a given time frame. This makes time management of utmost concern for any woman seeking to go into business and succeed at it!

There are as many time-wasters in any given day as there are minutes! I'm thoroughly convinced of that. A person can always find "something" that seems interesting or intriguing or enticing—more so than the *work* they know is required to build a business.

I recently read a post on a Facebook page of a young woman who is a free-lance writer. She said, "Note to self. Turn off Facebook and start writing."

As much as the social media is not only used, but *praised* as a good thing in our culture, it can also be a tremendous time-waster. I also believe it gives many people a false sense of truly connecting with others, when in truth, *connection* happens in dialog, not monolog, and the best connections still happen face-to-face. I am a big fan of Skype video chats and "Face Time" technologies. They are major ways I stay in touch with my business colleagues in many nations. I *use* the technology at hand to build relationships, answer questions, and resolve problems. I don't go to social media to troll for gossip or to give myself a sense that I am more informed about my friends than I truly am!

I am not criticizing those who feel a *need* for more people in their lives. We all need friends—real friends. We all need to stay in touch with our beloved family members. My position is this: Turn off the electronic devices and venture out to meet and make real friends and have real conversations with them. Set up times to *be* with family members for longer than a one-minute text message. You may not be able to drive over to a family member's house, but you can have a conversation by phone or Skype that "meanders" without an agenda. And the same goes for developing real customers and real recruits to your business. Life in real-time is so much more satisfying than life in a virtual world.

You may not have seriously calculated just how much time you are spending on social media outlets. Most people underestimate this time, just as most people underestimate the amount of time they watch television or surf the Internet. "Oh, I only watch a half hour of TV a day. I only spend a few minutes on the net." *Really?*

Some people I know *live* in their e-mail—it is always on, always "dinging" a new message, and by always, I mean 24/7/52. ALL the time! Get real about your time management in this area!

Statistics tell us that the average adult American spends *hours* a day on the Internet or watching television—for social reasons. And, at the end of that time, they have virtually *nothing* productive to show for their time. They cannot remember more than one or two statements of fact, and don't feel particularly "closer" to a person with whom they desire a close relationship.

There are people who need to be on the Internet as a part of their doing business—it is a great vehicle for sending out business reminders, sharing motivational messages to members of a team, providing progress reports, sending statements to be considered for a business proposal, or issuing a meeting agenda. It is a prime vehicle for processing orders and giving brief updates about them. I am all in favor of using technology to further one's business. But ... be aware that the tendency for many people is to veer off the road and spend time meandering through a high volume of information that has little to *nothing* to do with their work. They are looking for a diversion *from* work, not a particular piece of information that can compel them to succeed faster or do higher quality work. Ask yourself, "WHY do I spend the time I spend on social media or on the Internet? What am I gaining from it—truly *gaining* personally and professionally? What could I be doing *instead?*"

Setting Goals—for Both Money and Work

When a person decides to paint a room, it seems almost inevitable that the person will begin to think about purchasing new furniture. A refurbished room cries out for new furniture.

The same is true for our minds. When we decide that we are going to adopt new goals, we nearly always find ourselves facing the need for some new mental *habits*.

A goal sends a signal that we want to "go somewhere" in life. And that means we need to get rid of that apathy chair—the "laziness" chair or the "do-nothing" chair that we have been resting in without moving. We may have been in that mental chair for a long time—feeling comfortable, but not achieving anything. And we suddenly know that if we truly are going to "get with it" in our life, we are going to have to exert some energy and take a few risks. We need to GET UP AND GET MOVING.

A goal also causes us to look for new outlets, or new opportunities. You may have been mentally in a room with closed doors and windows encased in heavy drapery. It is time to open those doors and draw those drapes! We need to OPEN OUR MINDS TO NEW OPPORTUNITIES.

A goal will compel you to do something that requires *mental activity*—something creative, something proactive, something problem solving. You aren't going to find that in a dark, closed room with a television set for light, or a computer screen devoted to playing a mindless game. A goal invites you to be creative and to trade in a set routine for new associations and activities. In nearly all cases, that means reaching out to new *people*—inviting them into your mental space and seeking to learn from them in the area of their expertise. A goal causes us to REACH OUT TO NEW PEOPLE.

A decorator once pointed out to me the communication dynamics that change when a person shifts from arranging furniture so that chairs are side-by-side to arranging furniture so that chairs and sofas are positioned *opposite* each other. One allows for mutual observation, but the other allows for mutual interchange—a flow of ideas and facts, a rich communication activity that includes facial and body language. BECOME A BETTER COMMUNICATOR as you pursue your goals.

And finally, most people find that when they repaint a room, they nearly always find themselves *wanting* to add more light to the room. Perhaps more lamps or brighter light bulbs, perhaps new window coverings or no window coverings.

With greater light comes an awareness that there are parts of the floor or areas of the room that need to be thoroughly cleaned. The cobwebs and stains need to go! And soon, that thinking goes to the closets, shelves, or cabinets that might be in the room. They need to be cleared out and reorganized.

The same for our thinking. We need to bring in more light—new, fresh ideas and perspectives. We need to clear out our old ideas and habits that have produced fuzzy thinking, a lack of clarity, and little productivity. We need to clean out our "old data" to make room for innovative concepts.

Giving to Your Own Goals. If you have a genuine heartfelt dream, which you are translating into a goal with specific objectives, there is a lot of *giving* that you are going to have to do to turn that dream into a reality.

You are going to have to give to your goal—with all your heart and soul. You will likely find that you have a burning in your heart to see your dream materialize. You will burn with your dream, and eventually, you will burn *for* your dream. You will want to see *results*, almost at any cost, within the boundaries of what is moral and legal.

I have heard countless people through the years speak about business in disparaging terms. Too often "business" is blamed for a bad display of character or a decision that is a few degrees from honest or equitable. "Just doing business" for many people means sliding in whatever it takes to WIN in a deal—perhaps a little deceit here, a little fudging of the facts there, perhaps a little manipulating or maneuvering that periodically crosses the center line.

I don't want any part of that. And truth be told, I don't know any top-flight executives or genuine world-class leaders who do. The "great" people in this world do not compromise their values for a bottom line. And, they don't want to do business with people who will compromise. I realize that may seem like a lofty ideal. It is an ideal worth holding, however. And it is an ideal worth growing in your life and your business. It is an ideal that will yield abiding and wonderful rewards, far beyond money.

There is nothing inherently wrong or sinful about making money by working hard, and by spending money in honest, lawful ways. Don't let others discourage you for wanting to be a successful businessperson. Chalk up their attitude to "They don't know what they are missing, or could have accomplished." Keep on track with your own solid, honest, diligent work practices!

Meet Karen

My husband Arthur's niece, Karen, is an accomplished woman in so many ways. What I admire is how she took what she had and made a career out of it. As a child her mother had taught her to sew. As she grew up she pursued music education but got married before she could finish her degree.

Karen stayed home and raised her four sons. They are all married and she now has nine grandchildren. She and her husband Den have been married forty-eight years. Her husband's business acumen was a great help to her as she started into business for herself.

When the children were older and she needed some extra money she went to work for a fabric distributor. The owner recognized her talents and kept promoting her. As computers came to be commonplace she took classes and learned how to design patterns and publish books about quilting and sewing. She started a small business and became very successful in this field, all of which seemed to be an extension of the basic skills she acquired as a young child when her mother taught her to sew.

Karen's advice to young women is to get an education and always have an eagerness to learn. Keep up on what is going on around you in the marketplace. Her advice to you: Stay curious. Employ all the tools at your disposal.

For Karen, experience was the best teacher.

There is always a way through.

CHAPTER 5

May I Have This Dance?

*BOOTSTRAPPING:
AN ENTREPRENEUR
STARTING A COMPANY
WITH VERY LITTLE CAPITAL

"There are no shortcuts to any place worth going."

Beverly Sills (1929–2007)
American Opera Singer and
Manager of the New York City Opera

Business is an upward push, and it is a matter rooted in solid principles related to money and work. But let's look at it from another angle: Business can be a huge amount of fun!

Business can have the aura of adventure, and of personal challenge. That certainly has been the case for me.

In many ways, I was the child who was always looking for the line that somebody had drawn in the sand, daring me to cross it. I wanted to take that dare and reposition the line!

One of my greatest sparring partners was a long-term substitute teacher that was put in charge of my fifth-grade classroom. She was rich, bored with her life, and in my eyes, easily "moved." I sized her up within minutes and realized that I was as tall as she was. So one day shortly after she arrived in my classroom I said, "Miss Stevens, I'm going to wear your coat out to recess." This woman wore a full-length mink coat to my elementary school every day, and when she didn't say I shouldn't or couldn't wear her coat, I availed myself of the opportunity! I wore her coat out to the gravel playground to play kickball and she never said a word about it before, during, or after recess was over.

Well, if you give a strong-willed child an inch, of course she is going to take a mile!

A few days later as we lined up to leave our classroom and head for the cafeteria, I said, "Miss Stevens, I bet I could pick you up and carry you." She said, "Oh no, you can't do that. How would it look for you to do that since I'm the teacher and you're a student?" I paid no attention. I looked out into the hall and then grabbed her around the waist, picked her up and carried her down the hall toward the cafeteria. I remember the sixth-grade teacher, whose classroom was at the end of the hall,

81

coming out just as I walked by carrying Miss Stevens. She peered at me over her glasses and said calmly but seriously, "I'm going to retire before next year."

During those days, I attended a very conservative church, and the people in that church did not believe in dancing, smoking, or chewing, and they didn't want "nice" girls to hang out with people who did those things. Well, I was invited to a birthday party at a very wealthy boy's home, and I was both excited and nervous about that opportunity. I heard there was going to be dancing but I never mentioned that to my parents. I just went to the party and decided I'd dance if I had the chance.

I had learned from a friend how to do the two-step to a song called "Long, Long Ago." And that night, I fell in love for the first time dancing to that very song with a boy named Buzz. He had curly blond hair but the real miracle was that he was as tall as I was—even in the fifth grade! I couldn't believe how much fun it was to dance with a boy who was tall and good-looking. I decided that it might be fun to repeat that experience.

The next day when all of the other students in my class went out to recess, I stayed behind and rearranged the desks in the classroom. I pushed them all over to one wall and when Miss Stevens and the other thirty-plus students came in from recess, the teacher asked me, "Beverly, what is this?" I said we were going to have a dance. She asked, "Would it be all right if we had spelling first?" I reluctantly agreed, but as soon as she had started her spelling lesson, I headed out the door and walked to the principal's office, where I announced that I needed to use the telephone to make a call that Miss Stevens wanted me to make. I was given the phone and called our "room mother" for the fifth grade and told her that Miss Stevens wanted her to come to the school immediately and bring a record player, some Cokes and cookies, and some records, including "Long, Long Ago." She arrived just in time.

Let me assure you that if my mother and father had known what was going on, I wouldn't be alive today to write all this for you. My parents were strong and strict and I knew where the line was drawn with them, and also knew that I didn't dare cross it. But they weren't at my school or in my fifth-grade classroom!

Frankly, I'm glad I was a strong-willed child with a desire to have more, do more, and be more. That attitude got me into some trouble through the years, but it also got me to where I am today. If you have a strong-willed child, hang on and don't give in.

Did we have a dance that day in my fifth-grade classroom? You bet. We had a dance for the rest of the school day! It was one of the best days of my entire elementary school experience, and I have a strong hunch that every other student in my class still remembers that day with a big smile.

Basic Business Dance Steps

There are some wonderful metaphors that link business and dancing. Let me share a few of those with you.

The Solo Dancer. At many dances in many parts of the world, you will find people out on a dance floor by themselves—perhaps a small group of women only, or a group of men only. Nobody is touching anybody—all are in motion, some with wild and crazy moves!

I never thought much after the first few years of building a business about being a "single person" in business. It was just *my* business. And I don't believe my clients, or my colleagues, thought much about whether I was single or married. There really is no advantage to either state. There is no "poor me" or "special me" when it comes to a person's marital situation. There's only the pursuit of the question, "Why not me?"

What matters is your business professionalism and your drive to build your business in a way that is legal, moral, and of exceedingly high quality in goods and services. A ring on your finger is not required, nor is a ring on your finger a hindrance.

If I had to choose between being "happily cool," or "always dignified," I would definitely choose happily cool. Frankly, I think a woman can be both. Happiness really boils down to joy—an inner quality that is not dependent upon outer circumstances. "Being cool" is usually an outgrowth of inner creativity. I greatly admire both the quality of joy and the quality of creativity.

Dignified, on the other hand, nearly always involves a compromise with what other people regard as "proper demeanor" in a given setting. While I have no intent ever to offend others, and I do value courtesy and good manners, I am not always intent on being "dignified." At times it stifles communication and thwarts "relate-ability," that rare quality that allows two people to connect, or an audience to connect with a speaker. I don't think I have ever purposefully tried to embarrass myself in public

… I didn't need to try! It just happened on occasion. And when those moments came, rather than feel ashamed or seek to withdraw, I have chosen to laugh at myself. I quickly discovered that if I laughed at myself, inviting others to laugh with me, we *all* had a better time and there was no lasting embarrassment or loss of reputation!

Looking to Be Asked … or Looking to Ask. Frederick Collins once observed, "There are two types of people—those who come into a room and say, 'Well, here I am!' and those who come into a room and say, 'Ah, there you are.'"

Are you a person who is willing to sit on the sidelines—hence, the term "wallflower"—or a person willing to walk across a room and ask a person to dance?

Making others feel *wanted* is a key to building any kind of business, or any successful business team. Business success often boils down to "reaching out to others"—whether they are customers, potential partners, or influential colleagues.

Think back …

Have you ever felt unwanted? I remember in school when teams were picked for sports. I wanted so much to be chosen.

Every person, I believe, *wants* to be wanted.

What beautiful words to your ears when your husband says, "I want you."

Or when a neighbor says, "I want you to be my friend."

Or when parents say, "We wanted you so much as our baby."

Do you tell others how much you want them and how glad you are that they are in your life?

Mother Teresa once said that the greatest disease is "being unwanted, unloved, uncared for."

She went on to say, "When I pick up some starving person off the street and offer him a bowl of rice or a piece of bread, I can satisfy his hunger. But a person that has been beaten or feels unwanted or unloved or fearful or rejected by society experiences a kind of poverty that is much more painful and deep."

Going to a Big Dance. People who are professional or competitive dancers tell me that they have learned the most about dancing from going to dances—and often, the really big, competitive dance competitions. It is there that they learn what *can* be done on a dance floor! There's much to be gained in motivation and inspiration, too.

I am a strong believer in a person attending motivational conferences and listening to or reading motivational materials—not just occasionally, but continuously. You never know when you will encounter one new idea that can spark a revolution inside your mind or heart.

Mastering the Basic Two-Step. One of my early mentors in business told me that business is a two-step process: one, learn to buy from your own store, and two, teach step one.

Teaching step one, of course, means developing someone who can sell products in an organizational pattern that allows *you* to benefit, even in a small way, from every sale that other person makes.

There is a closely related axiom in business, a principle I have seen in every highly successful business that sells product: "Use the stuff, use it up, need it again." That's the cycle—over and over and over. If the company is a service-based business, then the variation may very well be, "Need the service, and then need it again."

This applies to everything from office supplies to home-cleaning services, from cleaning products to makeup, from air-conditioning filters to automobile maintenance.

In these types of business, it is possible to generate a steady flow of revenue.

And the good news is that MANY of these types of business can be done from a home office, which allows women to stay at home and raise their own children (rather than sending them to day care), and allows women to determine how many hours a week they want to devote to doing a business or growing a business.

"Doing a business" means actually managing the orders—both taking the orders and delivering the orders—and distributing information about products. "Growing a business" usually implies the recruiting of people who will become clients or partners in a variety of ways.

This also means that you PERSONALLY must use what you sell.

Any time you are promoting the use of a product of any kind, it is to your advantage to be a faithful *user* of that product—not just some of the time, but all of the time. I was acutely aware from my first days in "selling," that people who came to my home—whether the person was a potential recruit or just coming for a party—would be checking out my cupboards. Would they find the products I was selling in my kitchen, my bathroom, or on the shelves in my garage and laundry room? No matter what product line you may be selling, your greatest "advertising" for that product will occur when a person sees you *using* the product.

I regularly offer food-related objects that I "sell" to my guests for snacks or as energy boosters as we converse, or as we travel together. I don't have to say, "Isn't this great?" or, "Would you like to buy a twelve-pack?" Just by offering a free sample that tastes good and meets a need for good nutrition, the person is likely to say to me, "This is great" and "How can I get more of this?"

If you aren't linked to a company that has products you personally value and enjoy … find a company that does produce what you are proud to use and give away.

A Quick Retort for Those Who Laugh at You. Every person makes mistakes when they are learning to dance—they trip over a partner's feet, step on a partner's toes, and perhaps even fall down for no apparent reason. It helps to have a quick retort for those who may make unkind remarks, as well as those who have snide remarks to make about one's desire to *be* a dancer.

People nearly always appear to criticize a new entrepreneur. Don't let these people discourage you. Develop an arsenal of quick retorts.

- *You've been at this for a few months. How much money have you made?*

Answer: Enough. How much extra money have *you* made in the last few months?

- *Aren't you, as a professional educator, embarrassed to be in sales?*

Answer: No, I'm not embarrassed. I'm teaching a different group of people new skills, and showing them the way to a better quality of life.

- *When are you going to be able to afford a new car now that you're a business mogul?*

Answer: Soon.

- *How rich do you expect to become?*

Answer: I'm on a five-year program to becoming financially independent, and I'm right on track. I'm moving along at a speed that is comfortable to me.

- *What are you going to do with all your money?*

Answer: Whatever I choose to do. I'm looking forward to helping people that I currently can't help.

The day will come when someone is likely to ask, "Are you going to quit your present job and go into business full-time?" The answer may very well be YES. The good news is that you are likely to have a CHOICE about whether the answer is YES or NO.

Making Friends of Your Dance Partner. Many people who take dance lessons tell me that their partners have become good friends through the months and years. The same is certainly true in the dance of business. You will want your close business associates to be friends.

A business friend, of course, is someone you can count on being there in a time of need.

Be the Dance Partner Others Want to Dance With!

Most of us have been asked more than once in our life, "What do you want to do when you grow up?" Sometimes a person will ask, "What do you want to BE when you grow up?"

No doubt like many children—at least the children I have known in the United States and other democratic nations where freedom and "destiny" are live concepts, not dead theory—I was asked as a child both of these questions more times than I can count.

The person asking the question nearly always was expecting an answer that related to a profession. Actress … secretary … musician … teacher … nurse … doctor … Mommy … and so forth.

The childhood answers tend to change dramatically through a person's life. Indeed, in our world today, the professions many of us *thought* we wanted in our college years aren't at all what we are pursuing, or prepared for *today*.

Far more important, in my opinion, is an exploration of what a person truly wants to *be*. Not WHEN they grow up ... but now that he or she IS grown up!

Career answers are related to what a person might want to *do*. Character-based issues and traits that are beneath the surface of the "be" question, however, are often far more indicative of success than an answer related to a career-planning-and-placement test or manual. The person you seek to BE is the person you ultimately will BE. A particular job door may close to you completely. Certainly a number of jobs have disappeared in recent decades owing to advances in technology and jobs being shifted to overseas producers. The person you choose to BE is totally within your ability to define, develop, and manifest the "you" that you truly admire, respect, and seek to exhibit to the world around you.

There are specific character traits that I admire, and look for, in the people that I choose to call my friends.

Every person that I seek to recruit to my business either has these traits in evidence, or I have a belief that these traits lie dormant inside them—awaiting an "awakening" of sorts, and certainly, a "developing." My desire always is to enter a *business* relationship that *can* become a genuine friendship. That doesn't always happen, but when it does, what a joy!

Develop the ART of Dancing

Dancing in business is always enhanced by "better"—as in livelier, more engaging, clearer, more concise, and more artful—communication. Just as flourishes, dips, and a little fancy footwork can do wonders on the dance floor, so a little humor, a little candid sharing, and a little example or two can do wonders with your business presentations.

How you speak to others is as important as what you say.

Even bad news can be received better if you hear it from the mouth of a person who is speaking in a gentle, kind way.

Make it your goal always to speak with:

- *Respect.* No cynicism, no put-downs, no sarcasm that is demeaning, no name-calling. Address others and speak *about* others in a way that sends a message, "I value people. Every person has the potential to become more than he is, or more than she has."

- *A Positive Tone.* Every person knows the sound of bitterness—it is the voice of a heart filled with hatred, resentment, extreme disappointment, and in many cases, a heart that has been badly wounded but has never engaged in forgiveness.

- *Kindness.* A kind voice is one that doesn't need "volume" to send its message. Cruelty, harsh demands, and hate are often voiced in loud, bombastic ways. Tenderness is likely to be voiced in softness, even whispers. The one builds up, gently and consistently. The other can tear down in a violent outburst that leaves a person feeling shattered and trembling.

NEVER assume that people will hear you more clearly or desire to follow you more faithfully if you just yell louder. The exact opposite is true.

Give Concrete Examples. In telling others about your product and services, do your best to sprinkle your telling of facts and details with real-life anecdotes, testimonials from others, and fun illustrations.

I once was with a group of friends and potential business associates on a Yangtze River trip. We were moving along in a large sampan that had oarsmen. So it only seemed natural that we would launch out into a round of "Row, Row, Row Your Boat." The Chinese laughed and I had a brief opportunity to explain to him who we were and why we were in China. Have you ever had an opportunity to try to explain capitalism to a person who has never heard the word before and who has no concept to go with the word? He was enthralled with the little he heard and when I left the sampan, he was all smiles. He had a little "pig" that had been carved from a river rock and I asked him if I could buy it from him for one dollar. He quickly agreed. I said simply, "Capitalism." It was a living lesson, with its own musical score!

As I have shared previously, I once taught music history at the college level. As a music-history teacher I made it a point, as often as I could, to let "others" teach the course in ways I couldn't. As an example, when I lectured about Gregorian Chants, an early type of singing in the

Middle Ages, I *told* about it, and usually *sang* a few examples. Then we listened to a CD of this type of music. Then, I took the class to hear a choir or ensemble that was singing this music in concert.

Did they understand Gregorian Chants after my course? I believe they did!

Present a Successful Person. Sometimes the best "concrete example" is actually a *person*.

In Kiev, after I had spoken to a crowd of people gathered to hear about American business, a woman made her way to the platform to receive an award. She was very short and wore a big hat and had a huge smile. Someone translated for me. I learned that three years prior to this event, she had taken a train to Poland to hear me speak. She made a decision after that trip that someday she and I would be on a stage together, after she had earned the award she was being given. And there we were! Three years had passed and her dream was coming true. Of course I joined her in singing on that stage!

This woman was a widow. She had lost one child to death and had another child who was handicapped. She had been a teacher for forty years and had never made more than forty dollars a month. She was surprised that we wanted to take a photograph of her because nobody had ever wanted to take a photograph of her before.

She shared her dream with the people in the audience and she gave that entire audience a transfusion of hope on that day. If *she* could do what she had done, then everybody in the room knew it as a possibility for *them* to reach their dreams, sooner rather than later.

Having this woman on the platform was worth more than a half day of lecturing!

Use Humor. Not everyone can tell a joke well … but most people can tell about something humorous that has happened to them.

A few years ago, I had a wonderful opportunity to tell others how I found myself homeless one day.

I was moving from Newport Beach to Aliso Viejo, California. It had been a very long day of moving furniture, unpacking, and so forth. As I got ready to go to bed, I realized I didn't have my cell phone. I went out into the garage to look in my car and the door to the house locked behind me. I couldn't get back into the house, my cell phone was not in the car, and there I was, in my nightgown. I looked into the car and saw that the keys were in the ignition, so I got in and drove to an all-night gym and boldly went in and asked to use the phone. I called my son and there was no answer there—he was out on a date.

I then recalled that in my former house, I had a key in the garage and I also recalled that there was one couch that had been left behind (which we were going to give away). So I drove back to my old home and slept on the couch. Fortunately the phone was still hooked up so I called a locksmith to go to the new residence and open the door. When I arrived there a while later, still in my nightgown, of course, I just looked at him and said, "Don't ask."

Was this an embarrassing experience for me? In the moment, yes. But after getting several thousand people to laugh with me at what had transpired, all embarrassment was gone!

Humor can go a long way toward breaking down barriers, and also making key points.

Once I had begun to succeed in my business, I decided that all of my travel by air would be a lot more pleasant if I could secure seat 1A on any flight I took. That is obviously the front row seat in first-class—a window seat. That seat allows me to prop my feet up on the hard-wall surface directly in front of me, and there's usually a little extra leg room, too, which is important if you are six feet tall!

On one particular day as I traveled from Oslo, Norway, to Frankfurt, Germany, I was on a flight that had very few passengers. The business class was almost completely empty, and after the flight attendants had served our meal, they sat down in seats 1C and 1D to watch the video. It was a candid-camera-style video—visual clips with no talking, only a music underscore. I had such a great time watching *them* enjoy the video, and soon, all three of us were howling in laughter.

One of the flight attendants got up to serve the people in the back of the plane and she returned telling us that the passengers "in the back" were complaining about how loud we were laughing.

"What did you do?" I asked.

She said, "I pretended that I didn't understand their language."

I had boarded that flight tired and hoping for some sleep.

I got off that flight not having slept a wink and completely refreshed.

Humor has that effect. I look for it constantly. People are funny. I am and you are, too!

Meet Daisy

Daisy was raised in a family of eight children in Singapore. Her step-grandmother basically raised the children while their parents worked. She believed in strict discipline, punishment, and orders.

Daisy wanted out. She worked hard in school but didn't achieve what she wanted.

Her marriage at a young age ended tragically when her husband took his life. She was left with their two-year-old son to raise. She married again and had a daughter, but that marriage didn't work out, and they divorced.

Daisy faced a great deal of criticism from family and friends in her culture. She came to America and made new friends who encouraged her and she began a business of her own.

New hope, new friends, and a new life! She is now happily married and contributing to others' lives because of and in spite of her own sorrows. I am proud to be her friend.

She has taught me a tremendous lesson that a dream can carry a person *beyond* all tragedy and personal failures. A dream can propel a person forward and *upward*! A dream must be nurtured and sustained—it is often the only thing that a person has ... but if a dream is all a person has, a dream is *enough*.

In the pursuit of your business, find the opportunity to DANCE—with abandon, with joy, and with a dream in your heart that *cannot* keep you on the sidelines!

CHAPTER 6

Letting Go of Baggage

*BOOTSTRAPPING:
AN ENTREPRENEUR
STARTING A COMPANY
WITH VERY LITTLE CAPITAL

"You've got to make a conscious choice every

day to shed the old—whatever that means for you."

Sarah Ban Breathnach (1947–)
Author of *Simple Abundance, Peace and Plenty*

Years ago I read a story about a woman hitchhiking by the side of a country road. She was carrying two heavy suitcases. Two men in a pick-up came along and gave her a ride. They told her to hop in the back. After they took off they looked in the rearview mirror and she was still standing *in the bed of the truck*, and was still carrying the suitcases!

Sound familiar?

Any woman engaged in the "dance" of business will do well to remember that the dancer who is lightest on her feet is probably a person with a very "light heart" and therefore, with a "light-hearted outlook on life."

There is tremendous benefit to any person in life, and perhaps especially so the person in business for herself, to be able to set down the heavy luggage in her soul so she can move more freely and with greater joy.

Ask yourself today, "What baggage am I carrying?"

So many people carry with them continually some very heavy emotional suitcases:

- Past failures
- Disappointment
- Fears
- Insecurities
- The negative words of their childhood
- Bitterness
- Unforgiveness

None of these attitudes will help you become a more loving, generous, or appealing person. None of them will help you become more successful in business.

Some people have things in their emotional baggage that need to be "emptied out"—things such as harsh teasing, angry outbursts, accusations, put-downs, expressions of disloyalty, and hateful criticisms.

In an earlier chapter I shared about attitudes that I purposefully chose to adopt for my life. I hope you have given some thought to your own attitudes and the role they might play in liberating you, or tying you in knots.

Attitude is a powerful force. It is far more multi-faceted than "thinking positive" or "feeling negative." Attitude is an opinion about *something*. It results in a physical posture, often subconsciously portrayed, in a tone of voice, and in a set of behaviors, some of which can be very subtle. People in the engineering world have assigned a meaning to the word *attitude* that I believe also conveys a powerful concept toward life in general. Attitude is the "angle" of something in the direction of its movement. Attitude can result in a person soaring, or crashing. It can enhance forward and upward movement, or greatly detract from it.

Ten Key Attitudes

There are ten attitudes that I believe are absolutely essential for every person who launches out into a business venture of their own, no matter what type of business it may be.

Attitude #1: Have an I-Can-Do-This Attitude. Don't doubt or second-guess yourself. Expect to be able to set a goal and reach it. If you need to set a little lower goal than your initial goal, do so … but with the idea that you are going to learn how to reach this goal so you can set a higher goal very soon. The person who tells herself, "I could never do that" or "I wouldn't be any good at that" just voiced a self-fulfilling prophecy. Believe that you can succeed, and that you can *learn* how to play the business game and win.

Attitude #2: Have an Attitude of Gratitude. Be grateful for those who are willing to help you, teach you, and encourage you. Take in what they have to offer you like a sponge in need of a drenching. Voice your appreciation for the time people give to you to help mentor you and teach you about aspects of the business you choose. When you have an opportunity to introduce your leaders, sponsors, and mentors to others, do so with a grateful attitude and words of appreciation.

In like manner, voice gratitude to those who are working as partners with you. They are helping you reach a higher level of success than you could reach solely on your own. Be thankful for what they are doing on your behalf.

Attitude #3: Have an Attitude of Fortitude. Fortitude means that a person "sticks to it" without wavering and without quitting. Fortitude is a strength of character that enables a person to persevere, no matter what. The dictionary defines fortitude as a "strength of mind that enables a person to meet danger, bear pain, or face adversity with courage."

A person with fortitude will take responsibility for her own effort and perseverance. She won't blame anybody else if she doesn't make and keep appointments, make and complete sales calls, or make and deliver orders in a timely fashion.

Attitude #4: Have an Attitude of Rectitude. I realize that isn't a common word these days, but it means to have strong moral integrity, and very often, that is closely linked with a willingness to follow established procedures correctly, and therefore, to do a job in a way that a person's work can be "counted on" for uniformity and excellence.

I have worked with two types of people through the years: those who will "work a plan" the way it is designed to work, and those who think from the first day that they can create a "better plan" and therefore, don't need to follow established procedures. The people in the first category have a good chance of success. The people in the second category nearly always flunk out or bail out.

There's a reason for most successful companies to have developed their sales and marketing strategies in the way they have developed them. They have usually put years, perhaps even decades, into knowing what works, and what doesn't. After hearing a presentation a couple of times and trying to give a couple of presentations, you think you are an expert above all of the experts who have already succeeded before you? I doubt it.

Your goal should be to present information and techniques related to your company in a way that is consistent and reliable—all facts and figures fully verifiable. There is no "winging it" if you want to be a true professional who stands by her products and service, and who wants customers to "count on her" to deliver excellence at all times.

Attitude #5: Have an Attitude of Being Comfortable with Solitude. Being in business for one's self, or in business as a family, has a number of face-yourself-in-the-mirror and talk-to-yourself moments. Ultimately, the business will rise or fall on *your* attitude, *your* ability to self-motivate, *your* diligence in continually seeking new customers or new recruits, and *your* strong belief in your products and services.

I once had a woman helping me with the care of a large home who talked constantly. It took me a few days to realize that she wasn't talking to me or anyone else—and she wasn't delusional in talking to imaginary people. She was talking to herself in a very objective manner: "Now you've got to get in there and get those blinds cleaned up, and then you can take a break. Now you need to vacuum, and then polish the silver bowl on the dining table." And so forth. This woman got a lot done by systematically "ordering" her own steps. I rarely needed to ask her to do anything—she had already anticipated and commanded herself to get the job done!

All through the years of my business, I have found that I have a significant amount of time *alone* in my car. That's an ideal time to listen to a motivational audio recording, of course. But it is also a great time to have a conversation with myself. It's a good time to talk *aloud* what I see as the major challenges facing me, and to map out various strategies for addressing them. In essence, I have a "meeting" with myself.

I have also used time in my car to rehearse what I'm planning to say at a speaking event or in a small-group meeting, or even at an important appointment with one person. I have a good opportunity to "think through my thoughts" and speak them aloud. There's great benefit in rehearsing … in part, so you don't sound "memorized" later, and still present your material in an organized, calm, orderly manner.

Many people don't like being alone, or being silent. They cram as much noise into their lives as possible—always a radio or the television set on, always a hubbub of conversational noise around them or in the next room, always the clamor of life that seems to make them feel attached to the world. I strongly suggest you get accustomed to the sound of silence, and then, within that quiet chamber, take the opportunity to search your own heart and develop your own voice of *response* to various situations and opportunities.

Doing this is calming. It is motivating. It is a great method for *focusing*. And if your solitude words are voiced in prayer, it can also be faith building.

I like what the American actress Ellen Burstyn once said about this, "What a lovely surprise to discover how unlonely being alone can be."

It is when I am alone that I can see most clearly how I am connected to others, and what value I place on those connections.

Much of business is in one's head—it is a set of ideas that need to be formulated, put in order, and then executed. Much of business is "pre-play" that sets up a mental and attitudinal atmosphere that you control. Don't neglect the benefit of solitude!

Attitude #6: Have an Attitude that Accommodates Vicissitude. How do I know this word? I misspelled it in a spelling bee many years ago, so I have never forgotten it! Vicissitudes are the ups and downs of anything. Vicissitude is the inevitability of change, usually unexpected change, and it is a word that expresses the fact that nearly all things are "variable." They rise and fall, increase and decrease, produce and fail to produce.

A wise person in business never expects a straight line up the financial graph—the line is always jagged, with ups and downs that aren't always predictable.

There are five main points worthy of brief consideration:

• Don't let a downturn crush your dream and hopes. Learn to pick yourself up and dust yourself off, and move forward. Tomorrow is another day. Don't quit.

• Don't allow yourself to develop a "fear mind-set" that keeps you from making a call or taking a risk. If you become a pessimist about your own business, your customers and employees will also feel pessimistic.

• Learn to adapt and adjust. Business requires personal flexibility. Sometimes it is a goal that needs to be adjusted. Sometimes it is your own attitude. Sometimes it is a change in your routine, or expectations, or even the vibrancy of your voice. Sometimes it is a rebalancing of your enthusiasm and realism. It is a tremendous thing to be excited about your business and its potential. It is another thing to live in the reality of a future success to the point that you don't do the hard work required *today.*

• Don't beat yourself up over failures or setbacks. Assess the situation and take responsibility for what you might do better in the future. But don't take on a load of guilt or shame.

• Don't take out your emotional response to a negative situation on your colleagues, customers, or those you are recruiting or training to be part of your business. Stay positive outwardly no matter how bad you may be feeling inwardly.

This is not being hypocritical. Rather, it is being therapeutic. If you continue to project outward hope and enthusiasm, you will eventually convince yourself that the future can be bright and success can be achieved. Other people won't benefit from your negativity, and the greater truth is that you won't benefit either.

Vicissitude also allows a person to see AGE in perspective. As long as you can think and talk, you can be a success in business. That's my approach and I'm sticking with it. If you are a true pro, you'll find yourself getting BETTER with age.

I love the story about a little girl who was sitting on her grandfather's lap as he read a bedtime story to her. From time to time, she would take her eyes off the book and reach up to touch his wrinkled cheek. Then she would stroke her own cheek, then his again.

Finally she spoke, "Grandpa, did God make you?"

"Yes, sweetheart," he replied, "God made me a long time ago."

"Oh," she said, then a few moments later added, "Grandpa, did God make me, too?"

"Yes, indeed, honey," he said. "God made you just a little while ago."

She felt his cheek and then hers and observed, "God's getting better at it, isn't he?"

Indeed, God is!

Attitude #7: Have an Attitude that Embraces LONGITUDE.

Don't limit yourself to your *current location*. Always be thinking *expansion*. Set your sights on the next time zone. Even on another nation.

In the first few years of my business, a particular airline had a "package" that it offered to customers. A person could fly anywhere on their system for thirty days (the length varied over the years) for a set price. The price wasn't cheap—but it certainly was cheaper than multiple flight fees added together. I jumped on the opportunity.

This meant for *me* that I could schedule presentation meetings anywhere in the United States—in other words, anywhere I found someone interested in hosting a meeting for me to give an overview of my products, services, and business opportunity. For many months, if you wanted to find me, you should have started with my itinerary. Chances are I was on a flight going somewhere, or leaving somewhere and headed to another destination!

It wasn't at all unusual to find me passing through the same airport several times in a month as I crisscrossed the nation, developing contacts, trainees, and customers in many states—ones where I had never planned at the outset to have a business.

I encountered a couple not long ago who told me that they were thinking about selling one of their vacation homes. They lived in the central part of the nation and had a vacation place at the beach and a vacation place in a mountain resort area. I asked them, "Why?" They said, "We never seem to have enough time to use these places to good advantage. We are only in each of these locations two or three weeks a year."

Two or three weeks? I couldn't help but begin to calculate the number of home-based meetings they could host during two or three weeks, or the number of new customers or new recruits they might develop in each location. I shared the potential I saw with them and they looked at me in puzzlement. It had never dawned on them to use these properties to expand their business, which was prosperous but not *that* prosperous. Finally the husband said, "We could give you use of these places if you want to host meetings." I took them up on that! And I agreed to share my results with them. It worked out to be a good deal for all—and especially for the people who lived in these two previously under-developed markets.

Attitude #8: Have an Attitude of LATITUDE. Think beyond your current set of acquaintances. Who *else* might benefit from being your customer or recruit?

I know a woman who said she *always* has her eyes open for energetic, service-minded people. She often encounters them in restaurants. If she has an exceptionally good server, she always leaves behind her business card with a little note written on it, "I think you can be far more prosperous working with me than in this place. You've got tremendous potential!"

You will need to be forthright in *what* type of opportunity you are offering to people. Don't oversell the potential. But also don't neglect to point out the potential!

You will need to follow up on the contacts you make. My friend always asks the eager server, "Would you like for me to give you a call and set up an appointment?" More than half of those she asks take her up on the offer of an appointment.

Attitude #9: Forget the Platitudes. A platitude is a pointless, empty comment that is "announced" as if it has meaning or would be helpful. My least favorite platitude is one that is intended to be comforting, but never truly is: "You're doing okay." The truth is, the person is *not* doing okay or she'd have a smile on her face and a spring to her step!

Don't talk down to people. Talk *with* people.

Give concrete advice, not vague statements of hope: "I'm sure it will turn out all right" isn't a statement of hope. It is a wish that is rarely founded on anything that can be acted upon or pursued.

Offer a prayer if you are comfortable doing that and the other person desires it.

Reinforce your belief that the person has many wonderful, positive traits that can still be tapped into—and a future that *can* be brighter than her experience today. But in doing that, let the person know that you will be close to her side to *help* her remember who she is, what she is capable of doing, and why moving forward is far better than stopping in her tracks.

Attitude #10: Help the Multitudes. Any time you are feeling discouraged, look around. Look at the big world out there—with so many people in so much need. You can't help everybody, but you can help "somebody," and if you offer the right kind of help, you can help somebody, who can help somebody, who can help somebody, who can help somebody. You have a far greater opportunity to help the world than you currently know. In doing so, you will infuse your own life and business with greater meaning and purpose, and you will feel greater satisfaction and inner reward than you have ever felt.

Reach out. Make new connections that are beyond your comfort zone. In doing so, you likely will make a contribution to all of mankind. How cool is that!

Meet Else of Denmark

I was born in the countryside and my parents were very poor, which I realized on my first day in school. My teacher during my first two years of school did what she could to show me I had no value and, given my poverty, would never become anything in life. Rather than discourage me, I think she gave me something of an "I am going to show you" attitude.

Luckily for me the headmaster of the school gave me attention and really cared for every student. At home, my mother always encouraged me by telling me that I was able to do whatever I really wanted to do.

In the 1950s, my nation provided education for children until the tenth grade. My older siblings did not have that opportunity—after the seventh grade they were sent out to work.

When I was eleven years old I ended up in the hospital with a heart disease and fortunately, scientific discoveries about that same time allowed the physicians to rescue my life. Until I was twenty years old, however, the doctors kept telling me I would not be able to have children. My dream had been to have a family so this news broke my heart. You can only imagine how excited I was when doctors finally gave me permission to try for pregnancy. At age twenty-three, I gave birth to my son.

I decided to pursue a job in an accounting office and go to evening school for further education.

The course took six years, but I was willing to put in the time and effort. Four years into that training I got pregnant and postponed my graduation by one year. I did the last two years of school caring for my baby also.

Then, at the age of twenty-nine, I started my own business as an accountant. I did this work for twelve years—they were years of great stress and constant deadlines, and in the end, my marriage did not last and my husband and I divorced. I ended up in bankruptcy and once again, knew what it meant to have no money!

About this time, I began a new job in marketing and it turned out to be the best decision I have ever made.

I often have opportunities to give advice to young women who want to be successful in business. This is what I tell them:

1. Believe in your dreams and go for them.
2. Listen to your heart, more than you listen to the opinions of others who do not have your heart.
3. Watch people who are successful and learn from their example.
4. Don't be afraid of failure—think of it as part of the learning process.
5. When you get knocked down, choose to get up. It is actually easier to get up and try again than to stay knocked down!
6. Find a wise mentor who believes in you.

Else and Diane, whose story is told next, are two of the most courageous, fearless people I know—what a privilege to work alongside women who have emerged from such difficult childhoods to *fully believe* they can succeed, and in their success, be generous toward others!

I truly believe when you overcome your fear of failure, you are in the best possible position to pursue success.

Meet Diane O.

Diane was raised in a very fractured and dysfunctional home. At age eight, her mother put an advertisement in the local newspaper for someone to take Diane to live with them!

Diane knows from first-hand experience what she tells audiences:

1. Don't let life's hard knocks steal your courage, or DIS-courage you.
2. Believe in yourself and your potential, even if no one else does. This can give you courage to face obstacles that need to be knocked down.
3. Value yourself enough to keep dreaming dreams, setting goals, and moving yourself forward.
4. Determine you will NOT be defeated!
5. Don't let what you lack hold you back! You may not have the education you want, but determine to do whatever you can to get better educated. You may not have money, but don't let that stop you from working hard and saving money so you can move in the direction you want to go.
6. Don't fear failure. Two steps forward and one step back is still one step forward!
7. Above all, be *other-centered* and not self-centered. That will do wonders for your heart, and for your life. Develop the habit of being generous, kind, and loving toward others even when they don't deserve it. That will put you in a position to be blessed and rewarded.

CHAPTER 7

Team Advantage

*BOOTSTRAPPING:
AN ENTREPRENEUR
STARTING A COMPANY
WITH VERY LITTLE CAPITAL

"No one can arrive from being talented alone. God gives talent—work transforms talent into genius."

Anna Pavlova (1881–1931)
Russian Prima Ballerina

I would add to the statement from Anna Pavlova above, "And no person can arrive at success by being alone in her talent." As wonderful a dancer as Pavlova was, she was part of a ballet troupe, usually on stage with at least one other person!

No matter our field of endeavor, we all need others to help us, even as we help them.

In your search for a business of your own, I strongly encourage you to search for a business opportunity that truly offers you a sense of "freedom" to be all you can be, to earn as much as you can earn, and to influence as many people as you can influence! At the same time, I encourage you to look for an opportunity that allows you to work with top-quality people who are geared toward your same goals of business success. Choose to develop and be part of an active, vibrant, and rewarding TEAM.

Being a Good Team Player

There are several major principles involved in being a good team player. You may already know these as a matter of common sense, or as a result of your own experience. Let me remind you of them nonetheless.

Team Player Principle #1: Watch What You Say. I encourage everybody who joins any one of my business teams *always* to watch what they say, and be aware of who may be overhearing what they say—even if they believe they are conversing in private to their closest friend. Also ask yourself, "Is what I am saying going to hurt or help my business?"

You may say, "But what if the conversation doesn't have anything to do with business?"

The question remains. People will draw all sorts of conclusions about your *character* and your *beliefs* and your *motivations* in life by what you say, even in casual conversation. Their perception of you will spill over to their perceptions of the *work* you do, and also to the products you are selling, the services you are offering, and the associates you are training.

Never discuss performance problems or business problems with a person in a public setting. There are some walls that really do seem to have ears. I know, trust me.

There is very little to be gained by voicing any form of criticism or negative comment about any person, or any group. Keep in mind that voicing a criticism about your parent company is ultimately going to be taken as a criticism about the executives at the top of that company.

The person hearing your criticism is likely to conclude:

- If she is that critical of others, what does she say about *me* when I'm not around?
- Why does she work for, or with, people she doesn't respect?
- What are her ideas for fixing the problem?

Those who are chronic complainers tend to be people who believe that others should change more than they see a need for change in themselves. Chronic complaining produces pessimism—in both the complainer and the person hearing the complaints. Pessimism is like a big gallon of cold water thrown on the glowing embers of a new business venture—be it a new product or service, a new procedure, a new employee, or a new opportunity. What you "put out" with your complaint is often lost forever—it isn't likely to be rekindled because the person who has heard your complaints may never be able to get past your complaints into the realm of contributing new and helpful ideas, or developing compensatory strategies for working around a difficulty.

As competitive as I was as a child, I was no less competitive in my business—the main difference was that I cheered for *everybody* to win.

I went to the Olympic Games in 1996 and found myself cheering for all the racers, no matter their nationality. I admired any person who could run ten-thousand meters. I admired those who could stay focused on the track in front of them and not turn to look at the crowds. I admired those who had the endurance and perseverance to train for years just for one international race.

I feel about the members on my international business team the way I felt at the Olympic Games. I'm *for* each and every person to WIN.

Team Player Principle #2: Seek to Edify at All Times. There's an old-fashioned word that is rarely used these days—but in my opinion, it should be used often! The word is *edification*. It means to give instruction or enlightenment to another, usually in the vein of something morally or spiritually uplifting. To edify is to seek to "build up" another person in a way that improves their character, their reputation, or their standing within a group.

In nearly all cases, sincere words of appreciation and encouragement are edifying.

Always seek to edify the people who brought you into your current business, or who helped you attain the level of success you have attained. They should never cease to be heroes in your eyes!

Certainly edification does not mean deification—don't try to make the person into a god or goddess of some sort. People you are edifying are people you consider worthy of your appreciation, not your worship. Worship, by the way, literally means "service" in biblical terms. It means an all-out total-life commitment, even to the point of giving one's life for a cause. God alone is worthy of worship. Nevertheless, people *are* worthy of gratitude, appreciation, words of genuine praise, and sincere compliments.

I once read a story about two men who were junior officers in the Dutch Navy. They made a pact between them that any time one or both of them went to a Navy function, or encountered fellow officers in a social setting, such as a cocktail party or dance, they were going to take the opportunity to "brag" about the other one to those with whom they conversed. They agreed to do this for six months without fail and then reevaluate.

What happened?

They became the two youngest admirals in the Dutch Navy!

There were two principles at work, in my opinion:

• One, each man knew that he needed to stay at the top of his game in order to prove his fellow officer "right." Each man knew that the words of praise and value were going to be scrutinized by those who heard them—they each felt a need to "live up to" what was being said.

• Two, each man gained a reputation as a person who was positive, looking for the good in others. They both began to be consulted for ideas and for personnel evaluations—their edification of each other led them to opportunities to show their "leadership" skills across the board.

What worked in the Dutch Navy is likely to hold true in just about any organization of any size.

What might happen in your business if you had a policy of bragging on your associates at every opportunity—both those in positions higher than yours, and those who worked "under" you on a flow chart or organizational ladder? I challenge you to give it a try!

Mark Twain once said, "Little people will belittle you. Great people will make you feel great." Choose to be a great person!

Team Player Principle #3: Never Embarrass a Person in Public. I hasten to add, and never embarrass a person privately, either! It is especially important, however, not to embarrass a person in public.

Nobody will easily forgive your casting an aspersion on their character, work ethic, or integrity. If you can't say something positive about a person, don't open your mouth. If you can't build up a person in a genuine way with a genuine "good word" or compliment, check your own heart.

You may *think* your clever wit and sarcasm are endearing, or that people will know that what you say is a "joke." Don't count on it.

Team Player Principle #4: Avoid Special Favors. Overcome any impulse you may have to treat "friends" in your business better or in more favorable ways than the total strangers who seek out your training or your products and services. Never assume that a person who is a supervisor won't mind your requesting special treatment "just this once." And never assume that you are doing a person who is on your team a favor by failing to give in to their pleas to "overlook" that bounced check. Run your business like a business. Be honest, punctual, and precise, with *everybody* on equal footing.

Relationships Are the Heart and Soul of Business

You may be thinking to yourself, "All this sounds like so much Building Relationships 101."

It is!

Business is not about product as much as it is about customers. It isn't about services rendered as much as it is about the people you will help and the ways in which they will help others. Business is not about a big profit as much as it is about providing quality at a reasonable price in order to make life *better* for others.

If you lose sight of the people in the process of "doing business," you lose the heart and soul of business. Yes, businesses exist to make money, and in the corporate world, to produce dividends and royalties. But businesses exist in a grander sense to influence people and to help create a better way of life for all the people you seek to influence. If you get that big goal in focus, it gives greater meaning and purpose to the more mundane chores related to making calls, giving training or marketing presentations, setting up appointments, and doing the hundred and one other things related to ordering and fulfilling orders, choosing lines of product, or finding new markets to tap into.

Help in the Storms. I had occasion one year to go out in a seventy-foot yacht on Lake Michigan with my good friends Jerry and Karen. I asked the pilot of that boat about storms on Lake Michigan and he said with a great deal of confidence, "I don't worry about storms. We can outrun any storm."

I gained confidence from his confidence!

I believe it is true for most business "storms"—even the ones that blow in on the tails of a national economic disaster or serious business downturn on Wall Street. If you have a good foundation and are dealing with good, reliable, cost-effective products ... you can outrun the storm!

I have spent a great deal of time on airplanes in my life. Maybe that is why I enjoy *watching* birds as they soar through the sky. I never tire of watching them, individually or in flocks, as they coast on the wind. It is amazing to me that they fly *into* the wind any time they sense danger—and this technique carries them to a higher altitude.

That is one of the first laws of aerodynamics, of course—so vital to air transportation around the world. Flying *into the wind* increases lift.

What a valuable lesson for each of us to learn as we face the emotional storms of life. If we want to rise higher, we need to fly *into* the problem we are facing, with faith and optimism that we are going to be taken to an even higher vantage point. It is from "on high" that our help comes. It is also from "on high" that we very often gain the perspective we need to know *how* to face and overcome the obstacles that are hindering us.

Meet Sharon

Sharon is one of my mentors and a long-time friend. She is from Iowa but married a man from Canada. They have lived fifty-two years of marriage in Canada. I greatly admire how she has managed all the roles a woman is called upon to play.

She once told me: "When I was twenty-one, I had two children, born thirteen months apart. In so many ways, I was not prepared to be a mother, although I consider myself a good mother. I wish I had enjoyed my children more. When you become a grandmother, you realize how precious the little ones are. You invest in their lives by slowing down and enjoying the moments with them. I love all four of my children and my nine grandchildren equally and appreciate their distinct differences."

During her more than five decades of marriage, Sharon and her husband Jim have run a marketing business in many nations. About this venture, she has said: "Accepting people for who they are, where they are in their lives, encouraging them to believe in their goals and dreams, helping them understand how much God loves them, has been a journey for me.

"I first had to believe in myself, a shy, not overly confident person. But thanks to a wonderful husband, reading some motivational books, understanding that God's purpose for me was to support my husband in whatever he did and to be the best mother I could be, I became more and more comfortable with myself and my life. There is a saying that we are to bloom where we are planted and accepting that made all the difference in my life."

The Team Members Who Know More than You Do. There is tremendous advantage to your being a good team player with those who know more than you do! In most cases, in any organization, that is the person who has been in business longer and has much more experience.

Never be too proud to consult with others who are in supervisory roles, or who have achieved more in their business group than you have. Keep learning! Stay humble.

A man once said to me, "I was in business for twenty-five years and I did well. Why should I consult with someone who has only been in this business a little longer than a year?"

My answer, "Because he knows *this* business twelve months better than you do."

Sometimes the person who knows more may not be related to you at *all* in an organizational way. They may not be part of your business realm, or even be in business. Nevertheless, if that person knows more than you know about a particular subject matter, listen and learn!

On the Rwanda Gorilla Trek, one of our guides took a look at my shoes and told me that I would never make it on the trail wearing my Birkenstock sandals. I looked down at his rubber boots and realized our feet were probably about the same size, so I offered to buy his boots for one hundred dollars. He told me he wouldn't sell, but he would *trade* me for the day. So, I put on his rubber boots and he wore my sandals. I am so glad we traded. It was a very steep jungle trail, something straight out of Tarzan, and I was amazed that the guide made the climb in my sandals!

The Opportunity for Vicarious Team Members. The wonderful news in our business environment today is that we can learn and benefit from having team members who are often *far* more successful than we are, and who may live *far* away and beyond any opportunity for us to meet face-to-face.

Consider these people part of your *VIRTUAL TEAM*!

The fun news is that your "virtual" team is a team you can choose!

You can create your own "team" of people who will inspire you and motivate you, and be a source of both information and encouragement to you … and always be available to you! You will find these people in what you read, what you listen to, and the conferences you choose to attend. You don't need for them to know *your* name. You can make them part of your team simply by knowing *their* name and story.

One of my favorite songs, "If We Hold On Together," was published in 1995 with lyrics by James Horner and Will Jennings. The first verse of this song says:

> Don't lose your way
>
> With each passing day
>
> You've come so far
>
> Don't throw it away
>
> Live believing
>
> Dreams are for weaving
>
> Wonders are waiting to start
>
> Live your story
>
> Faith, hope, and glory
>
> Hold to the truth
>
> In your heart

James and Will may never know it, but they are part of my virtual team—active members every time I sing or hear their song!

CHAPTER 8

Educate Yourself

*BOOTSTRAPPING:
AN ENTREPRENEUR
STARTING A COMPANY
WITH VERY LITTLE CAPITAL

*"You can learn new things at any time in your
life if you are willing to be a beginner.
If you actually learn to like being a beginner,
the whole world opens up to you."*

Barbara Sher
American Writer and Speaker

I once heard a speaker say, "The biggest room in your house should be the room for improvement." A friend added her own corollary to that: "And the room for improvement should be a good *library*."

There are few joys as great as learning something new, and then, applying that learning in a way that truly *works* for your benefit and the benefit of others. The wonderful news in our world today is that *any* person can become educated. She may not have access to a great school, but she nevertheless can have great access to outstanding *teachers*—by means of books, DVDs, CDs, and guest lectures. Her education may not be considered "formal," but her education can be just as thorough.

If a woman is willing to go to a library and check out books and read them … or look up topics that are available on the Internet via a computer … or listen to information-based CDs and DVDs … she can learn a tremendous amount about the world as a whole, and about people including herself, and about any topic she chooses to "study." Yes, it takes guts and discipline, but I have told people around the world that if they will choose to learn, they are making a big stride toward a goal of overcoming all negative circumstances around them—first and foremost, poverty.

Truly, in our world today, learning is available to everyone. The obstacles to learning are there, but no obstacle exists that doesn't have a way through it, around it, over it, or under it. No obstacle is a sufficient excuse *not* to become educated.

Meet Dina

Dina is the executive chairwoman and CEO of The Dwyer Group. I met her at the Secret Knock Conference held in San Diego last year and we immediately clicked. She has answers for the question many women have asked for a long time: What can a woman do to create a business for herself and her family when she has no training and no education? The short answer is: get training and link up with a franchise company!

Dina provides training. The Dwyer Group helps women set up businesses in one of seven franchises: Air Serve, Glass Doctor, Mr. Appliance, Mr. Electric, Mr. Rooter, Rainbow International, and The Grounds Guys.

As she was explaining the process to me, we were having lunch in a beautiful hotel lobby. She looked over at the worker at the lobby desk and said, "You see that girl over there? She probably makes $30,000 a year. When she develops a business with us she can make $150,000 a year just by putting on work gloves and not being afraid to work with her hands."

Dina strongly believes that women are especially good at doing detailed work with their hands. It is not heavy lifting, but rather, *skilled* labor.

Dina holds to very strong values—much of her writing and speaking relates to themes of respect, integrity, customer focus, and having *fun* as you grow a company. I encourage you to check out her website and read her book, *Live R.I.C.H.*

I have definitely added her to my "virtual team"!

Seek Out the Very Best Reading Material

I don't know anything that can impact your mind as much as good reading material. I like what American novelist and critic Elizabeth Hardwick (1916–2007) had to say about reading: "The greatest gift is the passion for reading. It is cheap, it consoles, it instructs, it excites, it gives you knowledge of the world and experience of a wide kind. It is a moral illumination."

Consider the person who comes home at about 1:00 AM after a third failed appointment that week, feeling bad that she has no one to commiserate with her. She knows everyone she might call is asleep or still out with a client. She is too embarrassed anyway to admit to her mentor the lack of success she had that night, or that week. So what should she do?

My advice is, "Pick up a good business-related book and start reading!"

Reading will always change you—it will alter the way you feel about yourself—and it will give you an activity about which you can say in the morning, "The night wasn't a total waste. I learned something positive." Reading will give you a sense of accomplishment. It will inspire you to stick with your goals. It will renew and help heal the little part of your soul that has become bruised.

You may not remember all that you are told by a motivational speaker, but let me assure you, if you build a library of motivational books, you will always have a ready supply of motivation nearby!

No matter how many no-shows you have, no matter how many products are back ordered, no matter how many people you *think* are laughing at you for your pursuit of your own business (far fewer, by the way, are likely laughing—they may be puzzled, but at the same time, they may very well be envious of your courage or curious about your new goals) … no matter *what*, reading something motivating *can* renew your conviction that tomorrow *can* be a better day.

Make Reading a Daily Habit. There's a Charlie Brown cartoon in which Charlie comments, "Life's a lot like an ice cream cone. You have to lick it one day at a time."

Work requires a steady persistence. It requires effort over the long haul, and sometimes extra effort in the short run.

Building a business is just that—a *building* process. There are no long-lasting, reliable, get-rich-quick schemes in this life. I've known people over the years who have tried many of those schemes, and trust me, they fall apart very quickly in most cases. There ARE, however, long-lasting and reliable build-slow-and-steady schemes that produce an escalating number of rewards over time.

In my last thirty-plus years of being in business, I have advised people:

- *Learn a little every day.* This generally means listening to an informative CD or reading an informative article, or reviewing sales tips or marketing data that has been given to you. Add to your information base slowly, daily, and in a way that is incremental. Whenever possible, dive into a particular "course" of study—not a formal course or an academic course, but rather, pursue your need for information in a systematic, concept-building-upon-concept manner.

- *Seek to inspire yourself daily.* Read or listen to something every day that *motivates* you, or that builds you up in your character, or that reinforces what you know and believe to be the *right* things in life to believe, say, or do.

- *Do something every day that promotes your business.* It might be passing out your business card or an information flyer about your company or products. It might be sending out invitations to an information meeting about your business. It might be giving away an audio recording that tells others your personal story in business. It might even be a "tweet" or an e-mail paragraph of *encouragement* to those who work with you in some capacity. Your *encouragement* of others is a form of promotion—of them, and of your company!

- *Keep your schedule full.* Don't let days or weeks go by without meetings or appointments that are related to your work. I'm not at all saying that you can't take a well-deserved vacation from time to time. That can be vital to maintaining a good marriage or relationship with your children. What I am saying is that you can't truly grow a business if you are sitting idly by waiting for opportunities to come in hot pursuit of you. You need to be in hot pursuit of them!

Make calls and set up appointments. Call to check up on what more you might do to help a new employee or a new recruit. Note that I did not advise you to check up on others to see what they are doing for *you.* Check with them to offer yourself to them—seek to discover how you can help them reach their goals. As they reach their goals, you will benefit. But, if you make *your* benefit the priority, you'll lose your integrity and reputation with those who work alongside you. You'll also develop a self-centered attitude that leaves less room for genuine compassion and caring.

Here's my teacher's style checklist for you:

Yes   No

☐   ☐   Did you purposefully *learn* something today?

☐   ☐   Did you do something today that motivated or inspired you?

☐   ☐   Did you do something today to *promote* your business?

☐   ☐   Did you book an appointment today?

If you answered no to any of the above, don't make an excuse. Make a resolution that you will be able to answer with a yes tomorrow. And set out what it is that you will read, hear, see, distribute, or the names and numbers of people you will call.

If you answered yes to all of the above, you are one day closer to the top!

Read to Become an Expert on Today's "Trends"

As you read, consider yourself to be in pursuit of "research" about today's trends. Ask repeatedly about what you read, "What does this mean for MY business?"

Here are several trends worth exploring:

Trend #1: Self-Development and Training. Among the foremost trends over the last fifty years has been the trend of self-development. In the publishing world, the phrase has usually been "self-help" or "self-improvement." Just about anything can be "taught" to self, "applied" to self, or "removed" from self—emotionally, materially, psychologically, relationally, and spiritually.

Self-development materials are especially popular in three areas of life management: time management, money management, and personnel management (from how to win friends, to how to have a better marriage, to how to be a good boss).

Nearly all companies now have training departments, and a major benefit offered by some corporations is the opportunity for formal and informal education in areas that may or may not be directly related to a person's job description. In some cases, major training programs use a combination of books, CDs, and seminars. Most companies today find great benefit in helping their employees learn how to set goals and create new personal habits that result in greater job performance and high levels of self-motivation.

What does this mean for *your* business?

Trend #2: Personal Coaching. Closely related to self-development is the growing trend for a person to have a personal mentor or "coach." In the world of physical fitness, this might be a personal "trainer." As a former music teacher, who taught both in the formal educational system and also in the privacy of my own home, I know that "teaching" a person various life skills can be extremely rewarding, fun, and even profitable. In my case, the piano was already in the family room and was tuned. The students (a.k.a. customers) walked in with music books and sheet music that they had purchased, and I got paid. Not a lot, but something.

I have had friends who knew they needed to become computer savvy, but were afraid of "punching the wrong button." They hired a college student to come and teach them what they really needed to know, including the best programs and hardware accessories to do what they wanted to do. They wouldn't have thought of that college kid as a mentor or trainer or coach, but the role being played was just that—showing somebody else the ropes.

The best mentors are those who provide patient and abundant encouragement, instilling a "you-can-do-this" attitude. The good mentors and trainers also are people who personally practice what they teach. The net goal in all mentoring, teaching, and coaching relationships is change—positive growth and *change* that is beneficial to the individual and all who live or work with the individual. Mentors are always looking for win-win solutions for their mentorees, coaches are always looking for the development of a player who can contribute to a winning team, a trainer is always looking for somebody who can influence others to become walking partners or gym members or new clients for the trainer.

What does this mean for *your* business?

Trend #3: Lose Weight, Make Money. We all know that a prevailing trend in America, and in many other nations, over the last fifty years has been "lose weight, gain wealth." The Duchess of Windsor once said, "No woman can be too rich or too thin." I tend to agree with her and I find that most women around the world also agree!

So, if that is the desire of the world and a prevailing trend internationally, what does this mean to *your* business? Is it possible to do both simultaneously? Do some research on weight loss and nutrition!

Trend #4: Home-Based Activities and Businesses. We are definitely becoming a nation in which there is an increasing amount of overlap between "home" and "office."

I recently read an article that said nearly thirty percent of working women "sometimes work from home"—of those who do, more than a third said they work from home every day, and about twenty-three percent said they worked from home two to three times a week.

There's a second trend also worthy of consideration. More and more families are "staying home" for their entertainment. They are renting films to watch on their big-screen television sets and popping their own popcorn or ordering in their own dinners.

They don't want the hassle of going out at night—and in some cases, don't want to take the time involved in getting to an entertainment venue. For some it is a matter of not wanting to hire a babysitter. For some, a matter of not wanting to pay the high prices at concession stands (often adding up to way more than the cost of the "ticket" to see whatever movie is being shown).

More and more, families are seeking things they can do *together* as bonding times between parents and children. They are volunteering together, going on learning retreats together, or perhaps just "hanging out" together in their newly created spa backyards.

What does this mean to YOUR business?

Trend #5: Streamlined Procedures and Greater Efficiency. A number of recent reports are concluding that Americans want streamlined procedures and greater efficiency. As an example, I recently read that most products we purchase in an average supermarket pass through eleven different processes. For example—the fish must be caught (process one), and the can of tuna must be opened in our own kitchen (process eleven). If a manufacturer can cut out even three steps or processes without any loss of quality, productivity and efficiency increase, and so do profits. The more steps or processes that can be reduced, the greater the profits.

Always ask, "What can I do to make this *process* more efficient and require fewer steps?"

Trend #6: Use of the Computer. One main technological advance seems to be at the heart of our "at-home" trends for both entertainment and work: the computer.

It is almost unimaginable to our children and grandchildren that a time existed—not more than forty years ago—when the world did *not* have laptop computers, much less "tablets" and "smart phones" (which are also computers). Flat-screen, high-definition, and blue ray were unknown concepts, much less products. Many children today have never even heard of electric typewriters (much less ones that didn't run on electricity) or hand-held calculators (much less bulky adding machines).

More and more *business* is computer-based, and this is generally great news for the entrepreneur who is establishing a home-based business. A person today can do at *home* via computer what his or her grandparent couldn't have done in an entire week at a "real job" in an office or retail outlet.

Not long ago I heard about a poultry operation that is eighty percent computerized. The owners set thermostats and make sure food and water bins are filled, and they let the chicken house run itself … which it does, to a very nice annual profit and several weeks a year "down time" for sterilization of the premises and their own family opportunities to take vacations.

Many warehouses and delivery systems are computer-run. So are ordering and accounting systems.

If you don't know how to use a computer, you likely would benefit from *learning* how to use one—at least in the area where you can benefit from the precise, quick information a computer can generate.

If you aren't computer savvy or don't think you can become computer savvy, find someone to help you—someone who knows at least as much as the eleven-year-old next door.

[Note: A good place to find computer-smart helpers is at a nearby junior college; hire a student and you'll be benefiting both the student and yourself!]

126

Exploring New Product Ideas

In addition to learning more about today's trends, reading extensively will put you in touch with the "next big thing" or the "exciting new products" that you just may be able to fold into your business.

Years ago, shortly after we moved to Bend, we received the little poem below from Jim and Shirley, friends since college days. In their life together, they built a life-changing organization helping families. Their poem said:

"Ode to a Chair Lift"

How tuff it must be
to fish and to ski
or hunt in the fields with a dog

While all of your friends
your neighbors and kin
are stuck in this Gosh-awful smog!

But now you can go
with our blessings bestowed
provided you show that you care …

When you get up in Bend
and your spirits ascend
won't you mail us a bottle of air?

I'm still awaiting the day when people begin to package and sell "pure air." Who would ever have thought we all would be carrying around little bottles of "pure water"? Yet, we do. And when I am overseas, I am rarely without a very large bottle of purified water nearby.

I have no clue how air might be bottled and sold, but when it is, I'll send a bottle to Jim and Shirley, and I'll gladly sell that as a new product either wholesale or retail!

I started in a home business that gave me an opportunity to sell diverse products and train others to do the same. Over the years the product line has expanded many times. I hadn't *expected* those changes, but I readily embraced them. As the company expanded its horizons, I expanded mine!

Be willing to adjust. It is a part of what makes a business of your own exciting.

Learning about Money and Finance

If you are in business, you need to be "always learning" about money, and if you are engaging in international business, you need to be learning about international finance.

A woman named Sophie Tucker is credited with saying: "When a woman is 20, she needs good looks. When she is 30, she needs a good man. When she is 40 she needs a good brain. But when she is 50, she just needs cash."

I would add to that—if a woman isn't born with good looks and hasn't yet developed a good personality, she will *always* need cash!

Learn about the Value of Paying Cash. The great thing about cash is that it "goes with everything" and is your greatest travel aid. It allows you to go where you want, when you want, and do what you want once there. Forgot your dressy black shoes? No problem—go to a store in that exotic port and buy them! Cash nearly always works, and paying with cash often will get you a discount.

Learn about Investing. Recognize that you are already an "investor." You are investing your life into something. And you are investing in all sorts of material possessions—consider anything that you expect to have longer than six months a genuine investment.

I once read about a woman who used this strategy for investing in the stock market—she bought stocks in companies that had products or properties that she liked. She loved to go to Disney World, so she invested in Disney. She loved chocolate, so she invested in a top chocolate company. She was an avid photographer (with lots of nieces, nephews, and grandchildren to capture on film) so she invested in Kodak, and so forth. Her stockbroker was initially amused. He later was amazed.

There's a lot to be said for entering a business that allows you to earn an income from the sale of products that *you* enjoy using.

Learn about Good Cash Flow Protocols. I highly recommend that you read *Cashflow Quadrant* by Robert Kiyosaki.

Learn about Business Cycles. Your business is likely to develop in ways that will be an ongoing surprise to you.

Be aware that it takes *time* to develop a new business. In my experience, it takes about eighteen months to establish a new market. Often there is a quick burst of growth, which levels off and perhaps takes a dip, and then the growth re-emerges in a slower and often steadier climb. Knowing this overall market trend can help a person *refuse* to become discouraged if a downturn occurs.

It is valuable to know just where you are in a business cycle—as well as in your own life cycle. It will help you stay hopeful, and also be realistic.

Years ago, I encountered a set of paintings at the Smithsonian in Washington, D.C., that came to mean a great deal to me. They were created by Thomas Cole and are called *The Voyage of Life*.

I first saw these paintings when I went to Washington for the first inauguration of Ronald Reagan. I went with my good friends, Shirley and Jim. They had tickets that allowed them to invite guests, and I was quite happy to be one of those guests!

In one gallery of the Smithsonian, I came face-to-face with Thomas Cole's paintings.

The first painting depicts the beginning of life. You can see an angel, a baby, and a full hourglass coming out of a cave. All the potential of life is present.

The next painting shows a young person alone in the boat. He has set aside the angel as he pursues his own dreams—the sky has a vision of a castle. The young person is obviously looking ahead to a future in which anything is possible. He does not see the whitewater around the next bend. The hourglass is down a little.

The third painting shows the young man in the boat about to go over a waterfall. The angel is missing. The sky is filled with dark clouds that speak of debt, depression, fear, worry, and old age. The sand is sliding through the hourglass at a rapid rate.

In the final painting, the boat is broken up, the hourglass is gone, the man is old and gray. His arms are outstretched and his face looks upward. We see angels in the heavens coming to take him home.

I bought copies of these paintings to hang in the entry room of my home. For many years, they provided a good "conversation starter" as I asked various ones, "Where are you?" The paintings are not only a description of life, but of anything that "has a life"—which includes a business. Every business has a voyage of life that we are wise to recognize.

Unlike physical life, the business voyage of life is one that we can influence greatly. We can choose to stay in paintings number one and number two! We need to keep the angels in the picture and look out for the rapids as we pursue our dreams.

Reading for Inspiration

Beyond the world of reading for information lies the world of reading to learn facts, identify trends, and find supportive data. This type of "education" can do as much for you as reading to learn facts, trends, and find supportive data.

I strongly encourage you to read the stories of women who have "been there, done that"—and have displayed tremendous personal courage and fortitude.

One of the most inspirational women I have ever met was Alicia Jurman. She wrote a book titled *Alicia: My Story* in the late 1980s. I couldn't put it down once I started reading it. The book told of her survival as a young Jewish girl during World War II. I found a phone number for her at the back of the book, called her, and had a very good conversation—which left me in tears. I invited her to speak at one of my business conventions. She spoke to ten thousand people in the Long Beach Arena and I sang to her the song "You'll Never Walk Alone" after she had finished her presentation. I invited her again for a function in Anaheim, and also arranged for her to speak to a large group of children about what it was like to go through the persecution of World War II as a young girl.

I asked Alicia what she would say to young people today and she gave me these tips:

1. Get an education and appreciate the fact that you *can* get an education.

2. Stay informed about what is happening on the political scene in your nation. What happened in my life *can* happen in yours.

3. Encourage the young people you know to do all they can do to make our world a better place.

Alicia told me that she got up every morning after she learned that her entire family had died, and she looked herself in the mirror and said, "Alicia, you have to get up. *Someone* needs you today."

I have thought of that statement countless times through the years, especially at times when I may have been a little discouraged or wondered if my life would have any lasting impact. "Of course it does," Alicia would have said. We are all here at God's design and plan!

Meet Pat

Pat is one of my long-time friends who has been in business for herself for many years. "Starting a business" was one of her early goals in life—along with getting an education, marrying a good man, traveling the world, and having a family. The eldest of eleven children, she grew up in a well-educated, hard-working family, and as a teenager, managed to stay out of the drug-and-party culture that was popular at the time she went to college. She worked to pay for her tuition, room, and board.

Actually, Pat began working when she was twelve years old, cleaning houses. She also worked as a babysitter and nanny, a waitress, and later as a dental hygienist. She doesn't discount any of those experiences. She sees them each as a valuable opportunity to learn to relate to different kinds of people, learn problem-solving skills, and learn to negotiate, mediate, and handle conflict.

Pat was never set on working in the area of her academic studies. Rather, she wanted to follow her talents, and to a certain extent, trust her intuition, be adventurous, and seek new opportunities that called on her to explore her own potential. She grew up in a family that believed a person should work as if everything depended on one's self, and pray as if everything depended on God. That was her mind-set and she stretched herself repeatedly outside her comfort zone.

When Pat found the business opportunity that tapped into so many of her interests and abilities, she was ready to go after that opportunity with everything in her. She had spent years studying international business publications and various marketing strategies. She was an avid investor and was interested in charitable and philanthropic work. Her business opportunity matched her foremost interests and goals. She didn't find that opportunity, however, right after college—in fact, she didn't start her own business until she was in her early thirties, but in her words, "You don't really know yourself until you enter your thirties."

Pat works today as a distributor for an international company in Asia, where she lived for a number of years with her husband. She has developed a great group of business associates there, but her work takes her to many areas of the world. I caught up with her recently and she told me she had just returned home after two months in San Francisco, Germany, Michigan, New York, and Telluride, which included three intense weeks of caring for an ailing brother.

I asked Pat to tell me a few of the most important lessons she has learned in her years as a businesswoman. I had thought she might give me three or four lessons, but she gave me twenty! They were all tremendous truths shared in capsulized form—I didn't want to keep any of them from you. You never can tell which of these might be "just for you" today. This is the kind of list you can keep coming back to again and again, and always see a new application to current circumstances and relationships. So, here's Pat's Top Twenty.

Pat's Top Twenty

1. Set *daily* goals.
2. Choose to own a business that gives you personal freedom.
3. Do your best to balance family and business—it *can* be done.
4. Make time for the people you love.
5. Carefully monitor how much time you spend away from your loved ones.
6. Never forget your family of origin.
7. Don't hold grudges.
8. People enjoy spending time with positive, uplifting people—so avoid being a "downer" in your relationships.
9. Say YES to high adventure.
10. Believe in your own potential.
11. Try new things.
12. Be transparent and genuine.
13. Don't be afraid to admit when you are wrong.
14. Apologize when an apology is warranted and ask for forgiveness.
15. Don't meddle in things that are not your business.
16. Refuse to be a gossip.
17. Consider your children to be the most precious gift you'll ever receive from God.
18. Live sacrificially, giving to others whenever possible.
19. Be ruthless about your calendar—only spend time with people who are "enrichers" to your life.
20. Nurture your friendships.

If you are honest with yourself, you'll realize that you can meditate on any one of these twenty statements for *hours*—perhaps as you drive from place to place, or travel by plane. There's much food for thought!

There's a lot to glean from her ... if you will.

Learn by Experiencing

As I have indicated several times, I *always* dreamed big for my children. I still do. And now I dream big for my grandchildren!

I want them to see more of life than I knew they would see from their front porch in a medium-sized town. I wanted them to have more experiences than a textbook could give them.

I don't mind telling you that I enjoyed the experiences I gave my children as much as they enjoyed them!

I was asked to be a chaperone for my son's high school choir trip to Washington, D.C., where the students were going to participate in an event called the Festival of Gold at the JFK Center for the Performing Arts. Before the trip, I had the participating students to my home, where I showed them *The Voyage of Life* paintings in the entry hall. What a joy it was later to take them to the Smithsonian to see the original paintings hanging there! I don't think any of those young people will ever forget that hour-long art lesson in one of our nation's finest galleries.

I accompanied a group of young men to Arlington Cemetery and we watched the Changing of the Guard at the Tomb of the Unknown Soldier. One of the young men in the choir had a father who had been a soldier in Vietnam, and he carried the wreath that day and laid it on the tomb. What a memory to see these young men standing in respect for the father of a friend, and in respect for what the soldiers of our nation have secured for us.

There was a time when my son Paul was assigned a project at school—on whales. His teacher told him that she didn't want him to go with me to Hawaii and that he would not receive a good grade in her class if he didn't stay behind and do his assignments. I went to meet with her. I said, "Excuse me. My son is going to see whales while he is with me in Hawaii." And he did! We chartered a helicopter and followed two humpback whales for about forty miles. Paul had lots more to write about than any of the other students in his class.

I took my daughter Debi with me on a business trip to the Washington, D.C., area. While we were there, we met with a Congresswoman I knew. I asked her if she'd take a few minutes to meet my daughter. She did, and the upshot was that this Congresswoman asked Debi questions about how politicians might reach the "X Generation" with a strong message about patriotism. I sat silently a few feet away while my daughter expounded on various ideas for almost three hours—with a Congresswoman taking notes. I was proud of her, and proud that I could give that moment both to my daughter and to my nation.

And, as you might conclude, I was learning as much as Paul and Debi along the way!

I strongly encourage you to surround yourself with experts and learn all you can from them.

Never Leave Intuition Behind

In all of your learning—which is essentially a rational process of observing, analyzing, organizing, memorizing—never leave behind one of your greatest assets as a woman: your intuition.

Intuition is not easily defined. It certainly isn't anything most people study or *learn*. It nevertheless is very real, and a key asset in business dealings.

I like what American illustrator and inspirational writer, Florence Scovel Shinn (1871–1940), had to say: "Intuition is a spiritual faculty and does not explain, but simply points the way."

Everybody has something going on inside them that you don't know. Every person has a problem … an ailment … a challenge. It isn't visible *most* of the time. In fact, if it is visible, we say the person is "acting out." They are acting in a way that displays the problem on the outside by their behavior!

The invisible issues, however, can be monumental. They impact every aspect of the business cycle.

In this arena, I don't know anybody who is better at discerning "what's going on" than a WOMAN with a well-developed INTUITION.

I am a big fan of women's intuition. Women as a whole seem to have an ability to hear some of the things that aren't being spoken, but nevertheless, are being "felt" by a customer or potential colleague. They have an innate sense about what is holding back a person from making a positive decision, and about the information that needs to be provided for a person to feel "good" about purchasing an item or signing on the dotted line. Intuition can be squelched if a woman doesn't listen closely.

I strongly encourage you to …

- Learn to be sensitive to body language, facial expressions, and to a person's tone (and volume) of speaking.

- Watch for clues in how a person moves and gestures.

- Listen with your heart to the sounds that might be related to tension, weakness, frustration, fear, or hidden anger.

- Do your best to discern what is *really* going on in the other person's life—be it a customer, colleague, potential recruit, or even a person sitting rows away from you in a large audience.

- Trust your intuition as a key factor in your decision-making.

    If it "just feels wrong," don't do it.

    If it gives you a joy deep within that you can't explain, explore it.

    If it causes you exhilaration beyond measure, step back and wait a little.

    Learn the meaning of things not said, the truth of what can't be verified with the five senses.

    Develop your intuition to work *for* you, not against you.

CHAPTER 9

Leadership 101: Listen, Laugh, Learn

*BOOTSTRAPPING: AN ENTREPRENEUR STARTING A COMPANY WITH VERY LITTLE CAPITAL

*"The dedicated life is the life worth living.
You must give with your whole heart."*

Annie Dillard (1945–)
American Writer and Poet

If you are going into business, you are going into a realm of life that requires leadership. You *are* going to be a leader, even if you don't necessarily want to be one, or think you can be one. Others will be looking to you for answers and wisdom, for a certain amount of training, and decision-making ... these are all roles associated with *leadership*.

At the very minimum, you will need to take on the leadership of *yourself*. You will need to command yourself directly and indirectly to do the right thing and make the right choices that are for the benefit of the greatest number of people you encounter.

There are several traits that I have observed repeatedly in people I consider to be "leaders," regardless of their chosen profession. I offer them to YOU, a Leader!

First, successful leaders develop good listening skills. Many people seem to think that an ability to "talk" is what creates business success. Top salesmen are glib. Top executives speak, and are heeded. Physicians and other health-care professionals prescribe. Good communication skills are deemed important for any line of work.

True—but the *best* communication skill is the ability to listen. Top salesmen listen first to what their customers want. Top executives listen closely to the data presented to them before making decisions. Good health-care providers listen closely to a patient's complaints before running diagnostic tests.

No matter what line of work or business you pursue, you need to learn how to listen and more so, to *listen* with *accuracy*.

I recently heard a woman tell how she and her husband had gone to a counselor to help them through a difficult time in their marriage. This counselor had them do an exercise in which they each had to repeat back to their spouse something the spouse said. Both the husband and wife in this counseling session had to repeat statements four or five times before they got a statement exactly right! They each were "hearing" what they wanted to hear, or were anticipating the next thing that *might* be said, to the degree that they weren't really hearing what was being spoken.

I have seen this happen many times when a person has attempted to complete a sale or explain a product. The salesperson has been so intent on their goal that they lose sight of what the customer truly wants or needs to know.

One young saleswoman I was "auditing" told a potential customer all of the reasons *not* to buy her product before she proceeded to tell the customer the good reasons for making the purchase! We had a long way to go. She told me she thought the customer would think she was more "honest" if she told the cons before the pros.

Plain and simple, don't sign on to a company that produces products you don't use (not just some of the time but routinely) or don't believe are the best available. It is only when you are convinced that you are linked to a winner that you'll find it easy to sell.

My first advice to her was to go back and review the training CDs she had been given that told not only the many positive features of her product line, but also gave a sample "sales pitch" to use with a customer. I wasn't surprised when she admitted that she had never thoroughly listened to or read the packet of information she had been given.

Listening. It's a key path to learning. And a necessary path before speaking!

Both verbal and nonverbal cues are being sent all the time in any conversation or dialog, or even in an audience-speaker situation in which a lecturer is talking and an audience member is sitting in silence. Learn to read those nonverbal cues. At times, they are more important than a direct verbal exchange. KNOW when you are connecting with a person, and when you aren't. A good book on this subject is John Maxwell's *Everyone Communicates, Few Connect.*

One of the key people I always seek to *listen* to is the spouse of the host person in a meeting. I have gone with a number of people who were in training with me, and sat quietly in the back of the room and listened to their presentations to see how they handled questions. At some point during the evening, I would sneak out and go into the kitchen where the coffee was being made and there, I tried to strike up a conversation with the host's wife. If possible, I tried to make an appointment with *her*, but in a casual way. My best line was always, "Where's the best place for a person to get a quality-calorie breakfast in this part of town?" When I was given an answer, I'd then say, "Can I treat you to breakfast there tomorrow morning? I'd like to thank you for your opening your home to this meeting."

It is over breakfast that I learn where things are really "at" in that woman's life—about her frustrations with her husband's work habits, her concerns about finances, her feelings of being left out of key decisions regarding the business he has roped her into, and on and on.

If you do this—in a quiet listening mode—you are likely to find that many wives who are married to entrepreneurial men have already been through one or more ventures in the past that turned out to be failures. The wife may have a very well-developed feeling that any personal business is filled with risks she doesn't want to take, and among those is the definite possibility that the new venture will cost her valuable time, require additional work on her part (which she certainly doesn't need on top of her regular job and her home-related chores), and will take money away from her family (and herself). Those are major obstacles to overcome and it is not the husband's sole responsibility to calm his wife's fears. It is your responsibility, at least partially, to address these fears and help the wife envision a *better* life for herself and her family, not a worse one.

So I listen ... and listen ... and listen ... and listen. Eventually I say, "I know exactly how you feel. I've felt that same way on numerous occasions. But what I discovered was that if I didn't do something to change the situation, the situation wasn't going to change."

Nine times out of ten the woman will ask, "What did you do to change things?"

That's the signal that it is my time to *talk*.

I learned early on that in most home-presentation meetings, it is the man who usually sets up the meeting and is excited about the business opportunity. He has caught a glimpse of the big picture. His wife feels dragged along for the ride and she's not very excited about having some strangers come into her home—and especially on a night when her favorite television program is on and she has no bologna for the kids' lunches tomorrow and no milk for their breakfast, and she somewhat resents the extra housework she had to do to get ready for the night's guests. (Notice that I don't just target women for my business. It is great to have couples, but don't forget, the woman is the key.)

Such a "hostess" needs a chance to vent and to express. She needs someone who will listen to *her* dreams, which may be different from her husband's dreams. She needs someone who understands her situation and who sees the talents she might be able to bring to a business, and how they might translate into real money and a better future. She likely has some resistance to this "new path" for their life, and she needs to be reassured that it is a good path that can truly lead to a place she wants to go.

All of these things are going to be discovered only if you *listen* to the wife.

Am I picking on women as the holdbacks to a new entrepreneurial venture?

No. But after thirty-six years in direct-marketing and motivation-based businesses, I am very realistic about who is seeking to start a business of their own, and what their expectations tend to be.

If a *couple* is seeking to establish a business—with the hopes that it will grow and become a self-sustaining, independent, home-based business—the man is usually the leader in that venture. If the *husband* is the initiator and he hasn't thoroughly discussed the idea with his wife, she is going to feel left out before the adventure begins. She is likely to feel resentful or nervous or doubtful, or all three feelings at the same time. She needs to be brought into the inner circle of the business "dream" before the first sales meeting in her home. And if not then, certainly before the second meeting!

If a *wife* is seeking to establish a business, she likely has her own reasons and own motivations for being willing to do the extra work and make the added sacrifices necessary to get the business started. Her husband is not a key factor in her decision to launch out. He only needs to agree that she can proceed with the business idea, usually within some mutually-agreed-upon parameters about time, space, and expense.

If a *single woman* is seeking to start her own business, she has clear sailing before her, and her real need—if she has never been in business before or hasn't started an entrepreneurial venture—is for *training* and for learning how to motivate herself consistently to keep up her momentum.

Different needs for different people. And when you factor in personality types, family constraints, constructing goals that are realistic, and learning how much information a person can take in before their eyes glaze over ... you are facing a real communication challenge. And the key is always to *listen, listen, listen*. That's how you are going to learn a person's personality, about their family, about their goals, and about the qualities that will be their best assets and the foibles or flaws that they will need to overcome as they start and grow their own business.

What about the corporate world, or the traditional organization-ladder enterprise? The same applies. The more a leader listens to her followers—or the more a supervisor listens to her workers—the more the leader is going to be able to tailor-make work for specific individuals, and also provide the most effective motivational strategies and presentation protocols.

Second, successful leaders are able to laugh at themselves and see the positive potential in all of life's experiences. A good laugh can keep the blood flowing in any relationship, including business relationships. Hearty laughter, genuinely rooted in something that isn't offensive, crude, or defamatory, can bind a group together. I am thoroughly convinced that laughter is one of the most unheralded "good business techniques" in the world today.

There are subtleties to humor and these are often most obvious on the international stage. It takes a while to learn what other cultures regard as "funny," or for people from other cultures to feel comfortable laughing with you, often fearing they will be perceived at laughing at you—and vice versa. Wade into humor slowly.

The best recourse for putting yourself *and* others at ease, seems to lie in the ability of a person to laugh at himself or herself. If a person is laughing at herself, she is inviting others to laugh *with* her, and a sense of camaraderie can develop that usually carries over into the world of tasks and "duties."

I love to laugh and people who know me well know that I enjoy life and laugh often. But that wasn't always the case in the early days of my going into business.

For one thing, I came into the business world from the academic world. I had been a music *teacher* at the high-school and college levels, and was also a professional adjudicator at choir competitions for about ten years. I had a quick ability to mark what was right and wrong on just about any type of scorecard given me. I was an outstanding music "critic"—I knew when someone came in on the wrong beat, hit a note flat or sharp, didn't have the correct intonation or phrasing, or wasn't following the musical instructions on a score. This perspective was also carried over into my volunteer work with church choirs and in giving private music lessons. I was a music *teacher* and I felt it my responsibility to discover errors in performance and correct them.

This doesn't mean that I didn't have fun with my students, or that I didn't enjoy my work. I *loved* a concert or recital in which my students performed brilliantly—I loved the applause for their sakes more than for my sake. But overall, I admit that I had a somewhat "critical" mind-set.

I needed to learn to do two things:

• *Focus on the positive more than the negative.* There's a huge advantage to changing one's perspective from a focus on "what's wrong" to "what's right." The people with whom I was working in a business model were not amateurs or "beginners" in life and work. They were adults who needed training and encouragement. They didn't need nagging or criticism to motivate them forward. Praise is always going to be more effective than criticism.

• *Eliminate all sarcasm and cynicism.* I didn't realize when I was in academia just how "cutting" many of the comments can be among teachers or administrators. Sarcasm and cynicism seem to be the preferred modes of humor. Perhaps this is because it takes a certain amount of intellect to engage in sarcasm and "wittiness." Perhaps because the competition in academia is so fierce at times that the only way a person believes he or she can gain a promotion in academic rank or position is to "undermine" others in the department. "Cutting" remarks are common.

I learned through the years that saying, "Oh, I was just kidding," doesn't remedy the negative feelings that come in the wake of a sarcastic or cynical remark about a person's ability, appearance, or performance. Far better to say nothing than to say something sarcastic.

I also learned that there is no such thing as "constructive criticism." Criticism *always* is negative. "Advice" might be constructive, but advice is much better offered at a time and in a situation that is not directly after a performance or presentation. Advice is only GREAT advice if it is given without any immediate reference to a *specific* performance.

People will always respond best to words of praise about what they did right, or about how much you enjoyed an aspect of their performance or presentation. Separate the "teaching moments" from the "appreciation moments." You can always say, "Let's get together soon to discuss strategy." You can always tell a person, "I want to help you get to the next level," as a prelude for giving practical suggestions on how to improve their business practices or presentations. Along the way, you not only will impart good facts, and perhaps even provide a practice opportunity, but also engender good will and a sense that you are on the other person's team as both a fan and coach.

If you recognize that you may have said something hurtful to another person, or spoken to the person in an unkind way, write a little note of apology to that person, or give the person a call. Do what you can to turn things around to the positive. If you don't respond at all, the residue of the negative comment will linger far longer than you can imagine.

Along these same lines, it is very important that a leader develop a good sense of humor about her own flaws, foibles, and failures. *Everybody* makes mistakes—both the seasoned pro and the newbie. Laughing at one's own self is a form of role modeling "acceptance" to others. If you can accept your own limitations and errors, openly admitting them with the goal of remedying them, you will be sending a message to others that you are capable of accepting their limitations and mistakes—with the same mutual goals of helping them become the best they can be.

There are two overriding principles related to being positive—both about yourself and about others:

1. *Be genuine in the compliments you give.* The only thing worse than a word of criticism is to give a *false* word of praise. Never tell somebody she is the "best in the world." In all likelihood, that isn't true and never will be. It is far more accurate to say, "You are really growing into your potential" or, "That was the best I've ever heard you perform." A person will always be grateful for praise and appreciation, even if he or she tries to dismiss the compliment as unwarranted. And, the person will intuitively know if you are exaggerating the praise ... so don't.

On the personal side, don't criticize yourself. Don't call yourself stupid, dumb, or a ninny. If you see yourself that way, or berate yourself that way, you are only reinforcing something negative to your own self, as well as to others. You may think you are saying it as a "joke," but that isn't the way your own subconscious will internalize your words, and it certainly isn't something others will easily erase from their general impression about you.

When others give you a compliment, accept it graciously. Don't make light of their good words. Receive them with a "thank you," and a smile. You might add, "I'm glad for your applause. It means something to me."

If others give you a cutting remark or negative criticism, you can respond best by saying, "Thank you for sharing. I'll consider that." Don't argue. Don't fuss or fume about it. Walk away with a smile on your face and, as quickly as is convenient, find a *positive* compliment to give to someone in your path!

2. *Be quick to say thank you.* A thank-you call or note is always appreciated. You don't need to gush or be exhaustive in your expression of appreciation. A line or two is usually sufficient. It is the fact that you have taken the time and effort to say "thank you" that will be remembered and valued.

Don't ever take another person's good will for granted. That goes especially for spouses. Never assume that your spouse *knows* how much you value your relationship or how glad you are for your spouse's help and support.

A written form of thank you is one of the greatest motivators I know—it can reap huge rewards for you personally, and for your business.

Third, successful leaders DO take time to enjoy life. I know dozens upon dozens of individuals who are at the top of their corporations or at the peak of their careers. They are hard workers who put out huge volumes of analytical research, public performance, creative ideas, diagnostic advice, or therapeutic help. Many people might perceive them to be "driven." This perception is usually rooted in an *assumption* that super achievers must work 24/7/52.

The truth is that nearly all of the people I know who are at the "top" take quality amounts of time off to *enjoy* life. For some, the time off is with family, for others it is "alone time." For some, the enjoyment is interspersed a few hours here and there in a given week or month, for others it is a concentrated two-week period of being completely unplugged and unreachable.

146

My dear friend Ruth and I enjoy getting away from the routines of our lives. When we get together, we forget about business and just relax and enjoy whatever a particular city or beach might hold out as spectacular or special. I asked Ruth one time, "What do you do when you want to have some just-you time to relax and rejuvenate?"

She said, "I put on my jeans, my sweatshirt, and my sun hat, and I go out to my Rolls Royce and drive down the highway until I turn off on a two-lane road, and then turn off onto a one-lane gravel road that takes me to a particular bridge down there by the river. I park my Rolls Royce, climb down the bank, pull out my fishin' pole, pull down the visor on my hat, and fish all day."

She's a catch-and-release fisher woman, and she really doesn't care how many fish she catches or how large they might be—it's the process of *fishing* that brings her pleasure, and along the way, she has plenty of quality time to unwind and allow creativity to bubble up inside her.

Fishing is not my passion, but I'm glad she has found hers and enjoys it!

Actually that's a key point. Whatever it is that you *enjoy* doing that rejuvenates you, is not just okay to do, it is *excellent* to do! Don't apologize for what gives you innocent pleasure. Always look for an opportunity to do it. I suspect Ruth keeps a fishing pole in the trunk of her car so she can take full advantage *spontaneously* of times when fishing is a possibility.

I have another friend who enjoys taking a half day to drive about twenty miles from her home to walk through a particular wholesale block of stores. She can spend hours looking at new fabrics—which is one of her passions. She is always looking for the most exotic and unusual upholstery and designer-gown fabrics she can find … for cheap. It is fun for her, and relaxing.

Yet another friend will go to a favorite coffee bar overlooking the ocean—taking a notebook with her, gets the table with the view she wants, and lets the waitress know that she will be there for two hours and intends to leave a generous tip.

She told me, "I don't feel that I *must* write in my notebook, but it's there if I want to write down something. And I usually do. Some of my best ideas have come at the beach."

Let me share a couple of practical bits of advice about taking time for personal fun and humor:

- *First, never allow yourself to think that your job or your presence is so important that you MUST be accessible at all times.* If you can't leave your office or your business for a few days at a time, then you haven't done a good job as a leader. Part of what you should be training others in your employment, or under your supervision, to do is to handle the basics of your job when you are not there.

That does not mean that there might not be emergencies that warrant a call to you. Make sure those emergencies are carefully defined—they probably should be at the level of death or impending death of a loved one. In those cases, somebody, somewhere, can usually track you down. There should be nothing about your job that demands that you be available at all times.

If you can't unplug—literally, unplug from all the technological devices in your life—you likely cannot unwind emotionally or physically. Both are important for you to maintain high productivity and creativity.

- *Second, fun is a key ingredient to all relationships.* Find someone you enjoy traveling with. Not every person likes every thing. And you likely will need to find a number of different people who can travel with you from time to time to experience various things you mutually enjoy.

- *Third, creating an atmosphere in which others feel free to laugh together and share a few minutes of spontaneous conversation can be hugely helpful to the morale of any group.*

Meet Kathy

Kathy is one of my business colleagues, but she is also one of my dearest "girlfriends." She is the kind of friend you have fun with, cry with, pray with, listen to, and pour out your heart to. She is of Lithuanian heritage and was raised in Wisconsin. She had big dreams even as a small girl to travel and see the world. She always thought "out of the box."

Kathy's family was close and each member of the family encouraged the others in all they attempted to do. Kathy always worked—babysitting, waitressing, and managing. She married and has been one of the best examples to me of how to be a good wife. She loves her children and puts her husband first, next to God. They have been business partners for many years and travel the world both for pleasure and business.

Kathy once said to me about marriage: "Marriage has been the hardest and most fulfilling experience of my life. Two people together with their God can accomplish all things. Valleys and mountains. Positively wonderful!"

Fourth, successful leaders are approachable. The perception of people who are at the worker-bee level in any organization seems to be that the people who are at the top of the leadership ladder are totally inaccessible, and therefore, should not be approached with new ideas or even a friendly hello.

That is rarely what a top executive wants! A keep-your-distance demeanor is rarely what a top executive adopts.

There is tremendous advantage in every business for leaders to stay actively engaged with the general population as frequently and spontaneously as possible.

It's out on the "streets" and in the normal venues of life that top executives learn the most about their customers. They see how people dress, talk, and how they relate to others around them. That's where they hear the latest jargon, see the new trends in action, and also discover exactly *how* people are using their products and services … or perhaps using a competitor's products and services!

Fifth, successful leaders are always on the alert for an analysis of the "FUTURE" for various items and services. They don't want only facts about new products and services, but an understanding of "where is *this* going" and "how will this impact what people will want ten years from now." They are Futurists.

Are you aware that in ten years, one out of every four people in the United States of America is going to be sixty years old, or older? What do people sixty and older *want*?

In most cases, they want *good service*. They want to be waited upon, with kindness and respect. They are willing to pay for good service, but once payment is made, they want to *receive* good service.

What will this mean to *your* business?

Most of the people in the sixty-and-older age range do not want to have to *learn* new technology—they want to be able to use new technology quickly without a steep learning curve. They want technology to be sensible and readily accessible—to the point that the "next step" or "the right button to push" is easy to find.

What will this mean to *your* business?

They also want life to move according to their desires for rest or stimulation, for group activities and alone time, and for physical activity or sitting quietly. They don't want to be herded or scheduled. They want freedom of choice. They want to be "independent" for as long as possible, and at the same time, they want help to be readily available at the precise times they need or want to explore something new.

What will this mean to *your* business?

Another futurist trend relates to time. Cultural pundits are quick to say that "time" is the new currency. If given a trade-off of "faster" or "cheaper," people will nearly always opt for "faster" these days. This does not necessarily mean, however, that they want less quality. They *do* want more convenience.

We once were a nation willing to wait a month for international news—which tended to be made available at the movie theater *before* the cartoons or short features, which came *before* the major motion picture. We once were a people willing to wait five days for the mail to come. Now, we want the news instantly, and we grow impatient if someone sends a package by two-day delivery instead of "next morning first delivery."

What will this futuristic reality mean to *your* business?

Will a person choose a nutritious snack bar that can be pulled out of one's briefcase over a sit-down mini-meal at a restaurant? You bet— but only if that snack bar tastes great, has the right amount of calories, and satisfies the need for nourishment.

Will a person choose a food wagon on the busy sidewalk with quick-serve items in the $2-4 range over a walk-in café with items in the $8-10 range (including tip), so she can spend *most* of her lunch hour walking at a brisk pace through the city park? Probably—but only if the food wagon is scrupulously clean and the food is tasty.

We have moved beyond "fast food" in our world today. We want instant service and instant foods and we want them to be high quality.

What will all this mean to *your* business?

There's a trend also that *young* people are looking for home-based and entrepreneurial businesses at a rate never before observed. There are a number of reasons—some don't *want* to go to college, and some of those who have gone to college can't find a job "in their field." Still other young people are eager to take on the challenge and opportunity of "doing their own thing" and building an organization according to their values. Many of these young people want mentors, but not "bosses"—they want people who will give them wisdom and insights into business, but let them make their own decisions, for good or bad. They do not want a corporate job, and have no ambition of climbing someone else's corporate ladder.

Furthermore, many of these young people have a *few* skills—they may be able to type, for example, which is a must in a world of texting, e-mails, and computing—but they are not *highly* skilled and they don't necessarily want to develop a "trade" or enter a "profession." They want to develop a business that is creative and structured "just enough" to lead to good results, but not a business that requires strict adherence to a long list of regulations and stipulations.

What will this mean for *your* business?

Finally, there's a trend for *lots of variety*, and the potential for individualization. Just check out the cereal aisle at a large supermarket. Not many years ago, there might have been only twenty different types of cereal available. Now there are almost that many varieties for any one cereal "type," (think small circles of oats, granola, or flakes).

People want mix-and-match clothing, and a bikini bathing suit top in one size and a bikini bottom in another size. They want day-to-evening-wear styles, and "no dress code" in the workplace. They want to be able to experiment with fragrances and with cosmetics, and not spend a fortune.

What does this mean for *your* business?

If you are going to succeed greatly in the next ten years, you are wise to study the trends and start innovating *now*.

You the Leader. You may be saying, "Well, I'm probably not going to be in business ten or twenty years from now." Perhaps not. But you can build a business today that can be passed on to the person or people of your choice, and *they* are likely to be in business ten or twenty years from now. Your leadership of yourself today can translate into a legacy you leave. You ARE the leader.

CHAPTER 10

Earning the Right to Lead Others

*"I suppose that leadership at one time
meant muscle; but today, it means
getting along with people."*

Indira Gandhi (1917–1984)
Former Prime Minister of India

I am convinced that the leadership of other people begins with a deep appreciation for the VALUE of another person, and collectively, other people. You cannot be a successful leader of people that you inherently distrust, disrespect, or dislike. If you are harboring any strains of prejudice—racial, cultural, sex, or age discrimination—face up to that and reevaluate your suitability for business, and especially international business. Your role as a business leader will put you in direct contact with people of all ages, both sexes, and many cultures and races. Get ready for that!

It is at the basic level of human VALUE that you will be most effective ... or fail miserably.

Through the years, I have participated in—and led—a number of what have become known as "ladies meetings" in various nations of the world. The meetings present a mixture of grooming techniques and motivational ideas to help women to build greater confidence, and greater enthusiasm for their families, businesses, society, and professional ambitions.

Some of the women who come to the meeting have almost lost their own sense of personal identity and value. They would be hard-pressed to come up with a definition for character, which they often perceive as a concept of self-worth that belongs to others, but not to themselves.

At the ladies meetings, we often begin by asking a person to write this sentence at the top of a piece of paper: "I am special." It is a simple concept readily understood and experienced by many American or Western European women. It is a *profound* statement, however, to most of those who attend these meetings in other nations, and I hasten to add, it can be a profound statement even to an American or Western European woman depending upon her background.

A woman named Radhika wrote after a ladies meeting in India:

> The sentence "I am special" spoke many things to me. I had come from a single-family setting and I married into an extended-family setting in which sixteen people shared the same house. I don't remember how it started, but before long, I lost myself and my personal identity. I began to accept everything from everyone around me. I no longer knew what made me distinctive. I didn't know my own opinions or beliefs.
>
> At the ladies meeting I heard several women speak who were in situations similar to mine. They told how they had come to the place where they realized that they did not need to *argue* for their right to be distinctive, but at the same time, they could be firm on some decisions in their personal life. They did not need to accept each and every thing they were told. I gained a new understanding about different types of personalities, and the ways in which people display different personalities.
>
> I not only gained a new perspective about myself, but also a new understanding of my husband. I was able to know him better. Rather than be resentful of the other people in the house, I saw the importance of our staying together as a couple and being part of the larger family— and at the same time, finding ways for us to spend time alone together without any outside interference.
>
> In learning these new ways of thinking about my family life, I gained new insights into *how* to help my husband in our business. I learned how to be a better role model and instructor for the women who worked with us.
>
> The more I gained a better understanding about *myself*, the more I found myself valuing other women, and encouraging them to discover their unique identities. I want to help *them* reach their potential, even as I work to reach my own!

Do you see yourself as special?

Do you see every person who is your customer as special?

Do you see every person you are attempting to recruit for any role in your business as special?

It is a *must*.

Meet Arti

Arti is from India and comes from a loving family. She felt encouragement to pursue her dreams from an early age. She earned a degree from Delhi University and held several positions in the aviation industry and software design industry.

After she married she became business partners with her husband. They are building a huge team of business leaders in India.

Arti gives this advice to young women starting out in business: "Have clarity about what you want in life … then find the right person to advise you. Be absolutely sure why you have made your choices and only after that, find the best person to help you understand how to go about achieving what you desire. If you are thinking about starting an entrepreneurial venture, you must train your mind in that direction."

She further advises: "There Is much more education required beyond academic education. *Life education* starts when we step out in the open world. If we close our minds to learning and to changes after our academic education, there is a good chance that we will be unsuccessful and unhappy in life. Always have a mentor in *life*."

Arti makes an excellent point about mentors: The best mentors are mentors for the *whole* of a person's life, not just their business.

Developing Your Leadership Style

One of the best books I know on leadership was written by Esther Wachs, *Why the Best Man for the Job Is a Woman*. Below is one of my favorite quotes from this book—if I could mandate it, I would require every person who works with me to memorize this and repeat it to herself often:

> Regardless of gender, today's CEO can no longer tap his or her company's full potential using a command-and-control style long associated with the masculine mind-set. With buzzwords like integration consensus, collaboration, and teamwork being tossed around, the model for great leadership is undergoing a major overhaul. The next generation of leaders will be those who can build a vision based on awareness of economic transformation, then help their partners and staff fulfill that vision.

Wachs calls the next generation of leaders she envisions "New Paradigm Leaders." She believes they will excel for three main reasons:

- They have strong self-assurance that allows them to stay personally motivated and take risks.

- They are nearly obsessed with customer service, which helps them adapt to market changes.

- They don't try to *be* like men; they embrace their feminine traits and use them to their advantage.

I couldn't agree more.

Meet Farah

Farah was raised in a loving family and was greatly encouraged by her mother that she could be anyone she wanted and do anything she desired. Her grandmother also was very involved in giving her this mind-set.

Farah's advice to young women: "Don't let go of your personal desires to strive for your excellence. Work with your partner, but always remember, you count, too. I was afraid of conflict and, as my husband and I came from different family backgrounds, I gave in a lot to his family's wishes. The females in my family were ambitious and strong, whereas it was the males in his family who were dominant. I had to learn to voice my opinions—with respect, of course—and to state clearly what I wanted and why."

Farah has a heart for helping abused children. Her vision is to empower young women to not give up, but to live a purposeful life. She is finding new and creative ways to pursue her dreams, even in a highly structured family life.

Farah has given *me* boldness in saying to women everywhere: Embrace your femininity *and* your uniqueness!

Choosing Your Dream Team

Certainly not every person can "choose" their dream team. A leader can't always hire the people she wants most. But, to a great extent, you can *develop* people to be part of your team and you can avoid people that you know just won't fit with you or others already in place on your team.

From the very beginning of my being in business, I intuitively knew that I was looking for people with specific traits. This may have been the result of my auditioning many people for choirs and other musical groups—voices need to blend for maximum effect. It may have been my earlier years of experience in knowing how to spot an obnoxious person a mile away. Whatever … I wanted a wide and varied group of customers, but when it came to *associates,* I wanted people who would fit well on my team!

I searched for people who had the seven "ideal worker traits" identified below.

Ideal Worker Traits

Ideal Trait #1: Ambition. I wanted people with a desire to be more as a person, and in the process, grow to have increasing influence and income.

I have realized in recent years that "personal ambition" is not valued in some circles. I have met corporate executives who make it very clear that they want people working for them who are "team" players, and who keep any personal dreams to themselves. They do not seek out people who are particularly innovative. They certainly want people who will go a second mile and work long hours, but usually, only for the sake of the corporation or their employee-group *team*. In other words, they do *not* want people with an entrepreneurial spirit. They want only those with a "corporate mind-set."

I disagreed with this perspective. I wanted people who were eager to grow individually, infuse their work with creativity, and have personal goals. I was not looking for corporate people. I was looking for *entrepreneurs.*

I believe that one of the main reasons I enjoyed teaching and leading music groups was this: students tend to be both idealistic and ambitious. They are on an upward track toward personal excellence, and in that way, they *are* ambitious.

I *wanted* to be aligned with people who had some get-up-and-go-up in their attitude!

Ideal Trait #2: A Strong Work Ethic. Anybody seeking to build a personal business must have a strong work ethic, and be willing to do a little sacrificing at the front end in order to reap rewards in the future. The person must be a self-starter, looking for additional things to do to enhance their productivity, level of quality in serving others, and the overall development of *their* future employees. Being in business takes *effort*—not only in establishing the business, but in growing it and managing it over time. The work never *decreases*, in my opinion, but it is always changing in some way.

The truth for most people who do have entrepreneurial dreams and personal ambition is this: Work is *enjoyable.* There is a lot to be said for enjoying the work that you do, and making a supreme effort to find work that is stimulating and fulfilling.

Because I believe these things about work, I wanted to align myself with *workers*!

Ideal Trait #3: A Basic Ability and Desire to Communicate. I wanted people who communicated well with people from a variety of backgrounds, experiences, and circumstances, not only their peers. (I knew this ability would be best if it included a willingness to speak to small groups of people, not just one-on-one.)

Meet Renee

Renee proudly calls herself a "baby-boomer." Born into a lower middle-class family, she was raised with loving parents who were married sixty-three years. She was her parents' first child, and was raised, in her terms, "strictly," which is not uncommon for many first-born children.

Renee ran away from her parents' home and married at age eighteen. Her goals at the time were short-term—to be the best at whatever she was currently doing. She saw herself as being responsible for her own life and decisions, and sought to make herself indispensable to her employers.

When she was asked as a child what she wanted to do in life, she always responded, "Travel!" She dreamed of going on wonderful vacations someday, and thought for a while that she might like to learn a couple of languages and be an interpreter at the United Nations. She studied French for five years with a vague idea that she might use it in her career.

Renee's parents were encouraging, but were not dreamers or risk takers. They were very hard working and taught and exemplified a strong work ethic. They encouraged her to work hard, but did not encourage her to step out and take risks. They were extremely careful.

Renee held a number of jobs in her early years, at a bank and then later in the financial department at a very large church. She took additional courses in accounting and business management, gained some experience in property management, and later went to work for an advertising and design firm. They were in dire need of financial and administrative overhaul, Renee's specialties.

From there she went to work as a business manager for a couple who had built a large business. Previously, they had hired someone who had mismanaged their business and even embezzled from it. She worked closely with their CPA to get their financials in order and then communicated carefully with the owners to learn their particular business model. Over the years, she worked with this family to replicate the business model they developed throughout the world.

From such a varied background, Renee has lots of insight to give women who are starting out in business. Her top statements of advice are below.

Renee's Top Eight

First, decide what you really enjoy doing, then structure your career path accordingly.

Second, don't be afraid to try different industries before deciding on a direction.

Third, don't be afraid to make mistakes.

Fourth, if you are knocked down, get up, dust yourself off, and move forward.

Fifth, learn to be a good listener.

Sixth, put yourself in others' shoes. Try to see life from their perspective.

Seventh, don't take offense. It is usually *not* about you.

Eighth, be an encourager.

Ideal Trait #4: A Basic Ability to Manage One's Time. I wanted people around me who were able to juggle a more-complicated-than-normal schedule. Being in business is not a matter of getting up and getting "ready" each day and then going to a job for eight hours on a time clock, and then returning home, dealing with the daily home-related chores and family-related responsibilities, and trying to fit in eight hours of sleep. That's the norm for many people.

Being in business generally means far more than eight hours a day, even if you are working from your own home office. It means that you are always on the search for the ideas and people who can help you grow your business. It usually means, at least at the outset, that you are doing many of the jobs that are segmented in the corporate world—you very likely will be your own secretary (scheduling appointments and writing response notes after appointments), accountant (keeping your own financial records), purchasing agent (ordering supplies), warehousing supervisor (even if that means three boxes in the corner of your garage), and R&D director, always researching and developing yourself, your team, and your product/service line. Yes—it is a juggling act, but for those who enjoy the challenge, it can also be very fulfilling.

Ideal Trait #5: Flexibility. By flexibility, I meant a willingness to set goals, make a plan for reaching the main goal and perhaps sub-goals, and then not be knocked off track if things didn't go exactly as planned . . . sometimes things go *better* than planned! And sometimes, worse.

Flexibility, from my perspective, included a willingness to learn some new skills—perhaps in business recordkeeping, certainly with the products and services being sold—and also a willingness to *grow* as a person. From my perspective, flexibility in a team member included a willingness to adjust a plan midway.

Ideal Trait #6: Hopefulness. I wanted people with an ability to be self-motivating and optimistic about the future. I use the word *hope* rather than optimism because it seems to me that optimism is usually related to external circumstances and situations, and hope is an internal perspective on life that is not bound to either current or in-the-near-future timelines.

Ideal Trait #7: Good Character. Above all, I wanted people who had a longstanding track record of being reliable, consistent, honest, and unprejudiced toward people of other cultures, races, or social standing. Add a dose of compassion and a dash of empathy to a person of good character and you'll generally find that you have an excellent person to work alongside. The person likely will be eager for your advice and help, and soak up every good idea you offer.

The Challenge of LEADING

Once a leader finds, recruits, or develops a team, there is a challenge related to the ongoing leadership of that group of people. That challenge has at least five facets to it. These challenges never go away. As long as a person has a team in her business, these challenges will be there! They are there for all types of businesses and organizations. Get ready for these challenges to be "permanent" in your business career, and learn to embrace them.

Challenge #1: Selling the Vision. A leader faces an ongoing challenge of selling the basic principle or vision that gave rise to the company and continues to fuel it philosophically. You may think that this is done by the time a future employee or partner is "trained." Not so!

Think about teaching your child to brush his or her teeth. How many times did you have to tell your child to brush her teeth, how to do a good job of it, and how to get to the point where your child was brushing her teeth because *she* wanted to.

Now apply this general idea to those who are part of your team. There is never a point where you will not need to reinforce vision, and in many cases, reinforce key aspects of procedure. This can certainly be done in a way that is more inspirational and motivational than dictatorial. It needs to be done nonetheless.

Challenge #2: Focus Like a Laser. Problems need to be addressed immediately and with laser-like focus. Don't be vague—you will only be opening the door to a concept that has been called "mental wandering around." Tell those with whom you work *precisely* what you hope to see, and the performance you desire for them to achieve *their* goals. If deadlines are involved, make them clear and give periodic reminders. This, too, can be done in a motivational way.

If team goals are established, remind the team members of the goals frequently, including the benefits of meeting the goals and periodic updates about a team's progress toward the accomplishment of a goal. Again, it can be done in a motivational way.

To succeed in having a focused team, you as a leader need to have a desire and a plan for *staying* focused personally. Become a master of scheduling and managing your own time, and of marking your own progress toward goals that are very precise and plans that are as detailed as they need to be to get the job done. Know how to turn your dreams into concrete *written* plans, with periodic sub-goals and an awareness of the tasks that must be accomplished to reach each goal.

Challenge #3: Become an Expert in "High Touch." We live in a high-tech world. People love gadgets and admire technological savvy. However, I believe there is something that people desire even more than technology. They like to feel connected to a person. In "touch."

Simple expressions of "touching" can be anything from a pat on the shoulder, sitting next to an associate rather than across a big table or desk, or engaging in a high-five or fist bump at hearing good news.

High touch can be a handwritten note on a beautiful card, a bouquet of flowers, or a visit to the hospital. Whatever is needed for that person to feel valued.

All of these small gestures have the potential to convey volumes about your care, concern, or support of a colleague—whether that person is above you, below you, or walking beside you in the business structure you have adopted or developed.

Challenge #4: Turn Every Challenge into an Opportunity. Develop a personal mind-set that every new challenge—often couched in terms of a new procedure, a new executive installed "above" you, or a new product line—has a unique and wonderful opportunity for personal growth and development, and also the potential for increased profits for the company and for each partner or employee.

This attitude will ensure your superiors that you are a willing team player.

It will give your team a sense of security and also motivation.

It will give *you* a perspective that will enable you to give your best to the new goals and achieve the most.

In many ways "high touch" is an extension of a basic intuition that many women possess. Women, overall, seem to have greater empathy and a greater concern with cooperation or consensus than men.

I have a friend who worked in the corporate world for more than a decade and she said of herself, "I approached my vice-president role more as a mother than a father. This didn't mean that I was more lenient, nor did it mean that I required less discipline or lower standards. Not at all. I expected the best and most effort, and the highest loyalty. But, compared to many of my male counterparts, I also was more interested in hearing what each member of my immediate team had to say—I didn't just tolerate their ideas or try to accommodate their opinions, I actively sought out their creative input.

"I insisted that my team members speak kindly to one another—no cynical or sarcastic 'cutting' remarks, no hurtful commentary, and absolutely no profanity or gutter language allowed. I refused to hear or encourage racial, sexual, cultural, or religious jokes. I demanded politeness and good manners. And I gave my team members a huge amount of praise and recognition for good performance and good ideas that benefited not only our department but the entire enterprise. Years later, I heard some of my former employees describing their years in my department as 'the best job I've ever had,' with a summary opinion that 'we were more like a family than a corporate division.'

"These comments were voiced by both men and women who had been part of my team. I was pleased at that. What I knew was that we increased our work output by thirty percent over three years, with a decrease in personnel of ten percent and no increase in budget. If being like a 'mom' worked—who was I to try to be a 'dad'?"

This woman, from my perspective, produced a high-touch environment—one loaded with expressions of appreciation and common-sense valuing of every person on the team. It was a department in which all other high-touch recommendations seemed natural, not feigned, and were appreciated by both men and women employees alike.

Challenge #5: Become Obsessed with Exceeding Customer Needs. Find out what your customers want in order to help them make wise purchasing choices; then find out what your customers have enjoyed using and provide more of that item and similar items.

The key to discovering what a customer likes often becomes obvious if the customer is given a *sampling* of various items—with an invitation to try one or more of the items. This works for everything from food items to lipsticks. Of course, a person who pre-samples an item has a far greater likelihood of *liking* the item purchased, and therefore, is more likely to repurchase the product in the future.

Challenge #6: Fight for Your Team, and Your Customers. If your team members or your customers come under the fire of intense criticism, or become the targets for layoffs, frozen salary budgets, or a delay in awarding benefits … fight back. I'm not at all recommending negative language or hostile vengeance. Rather, I propose that you find a creative solution that benefits all parties concerned, and present that plan in a strong, consistent, and persevering manner. Reinforce what the upper-level management of your corporation already knows—a business depends upon happy customers and willing workers.

Always seek greater understanding about a problem before you jump into action. Get all the facts, and to the greatest extent possible, get the truth. Truth and facts aren't always the same—strive to get to the deepest levels of meaning.

Don't allow others to snipe at or malign members of your team. Stand up for their ability and character. Always seek a "second chance." Always defend your customers' rights to receive the best quality at the fairest price in the timeliest manner.

There is also much to be said for a leader who is willing to voice new ideas—her own, the composite ideas of her team, or the idea of a superstar on her team. Take the approach that a good idea is a good idea, no matter who has it! Be willing to share any glory that comes from it.

Speak up for innovation that has a direct potential for increasing sales, customer satisfaction, or opening up a new market. An idea should have substance and a strong bottom line. It should be fairly easy to implement without huge corporate outlay or a large increase in personnel. It should be an idea that can be readily communicated both internally and to an expanding customer base or new market. Don't be intimidated by a person "above you" who seems closed-minded or highly resistant to change of any type. Couch the new idea in terms that address a superior's fears, and that give plenty of room for the superior to gain personal benefit from the new idea. In other words, make him part of your "team" and reward him or her with great appreciation and recognition after the idea succeeds.

At times, problems arise because old rules and procedures are in need of being retired or adjusted greatly. Changes in technology often allow for streamlining of paperwork—as an example, it's amazing to me that *any* company might still need forms in triplicate.

Encourage Initiative—in Yourself and Others. Whatever your job is now, as you dream about or are planning to start a business of your own, ask yourself, "What might I do where I'm at RIGHT NOW to make things better?"

Immediately after I finished my undergraduate college degree, I went to work for an oil business in Texas. The owner, T. Boone Pickens, was in his first petroleum exploration venture. He later went on to become one of the biggest oilmen in the United States. I was hired to work in the treasurer's office as a secretary. At the outset, I knew very little about what to do, but I watched, listened, and learned.

One day I noticed how difficult it was to file the many check stubs in the large filing cabinet set aside for that purpose.

I went into the supply room and pulled out the expandable folders they used to file their many geological reports, and I used those to organize the check stubs. You would have thought I had discovered a new drilling site. The treasurer was thrilled with this "new" innovation. He said, "I can't believe we didn't think of this."

Everywhere I worked after that, I asked myself, "What can I do to make this situation more functional?"

This concept of taking personal initiative is indispensable in business. There are always boundaries, of course, as to what you *can* implement in a business operated or supervised by another person, but there should be no limits when it comes to your desire to *think about* or *anticipate* the possibility of innovation and improvement. Learn to adopt this mind-set in whatever situation you find yourself—not only on the job but in other settings involving procedures, protocol, and systems.

And then, be open to accepting the innovative ideas that are presented by your co-workers or those who work under you. Be open to the ideas they have to contribute. Look for win-win situations. Truly, *everybody* wins when a new idea works for the benefit of the entire company or organization, no matter who initiates the idea.

Be quick to defend to your superiors those ideas that allow for greater efficiency without any loss in productivity or quality! Fight for positive change and forward motion.

Keep your "fighting" civil. Keep your arguments confined to a single problem or need. Keep your temper firmly under control. And be willing to accept the ultimate outcome—at least for a while, until you are able to regroup your creativity and energy.

If something is worth fighting for, however, don't give up on the long-range goal. The end is "not yet."

Embrace and boldly take on these six leadership challenges and your team will thank you with their best effort and highest level of results. In turn, you will experience maximum satisfaction and purpose. It's a WIN-WIN. But you must *lead*.

CHAPTER 11

Significance to Success

*BOOTSTRAPPING:
AN ENTREPRENEUR
STARTING A COMPANY
WITH VERY LITTLE CAPITAL

*"To give without any reward, or any
notice, has a special quality of its own."*

Anne Morrow Lindbergh (1906–2001)
American Writer and Pioneering Aviator

So many people are focused on achieving "success." They tend to define success in terms of what their careers or lives give to them—position, privileged status, greater opportunities, better health, more material possessions, increased luxury and leisure. None of these are "bad" things. To be sure, they can be very good things if they allow us to enjoy a greater quality of life, and to extend that quality of life to others.

But that brings us to the word *significance*.

Which comes first, *significance* or *success*?

My first two goals were outward—first, shoes and cultural opportunities for my children, then second, scholarships for young musicians. Both of these goals were about others who were dear to me; the goals were not *about* me. I believe that set me on a track for success as I expanded my compassionate and philanthropic dreams.

Before and after significance can come success if you follow good business principles.

Significance is defined usually as a life of great meaning. For me, it means:

- Living in a way that influences others for good

- Contributing to your immediate family, community, and home nation in ways that raise the "water level" for everybody (or for "all boats in the water")

- Putting your focus on things that are lasting and eternal

- Giving all aspects of your *self*—your talents, skills, time, possessions, knowledge and wisdom, and energy to produce organizations, processes, creative endeavors—in such a way that other people aspire to BE more and DO more

Success points inward.

Significance points outward.

Meet the Rilling Family

When I first moved to Oregon in 1971 I was invited to sing in a professional choir for a newly-formed festival in Eugene, a city in Oregon about 250 miles away from where I lived in Bend. At the time, I had a young daughter, no job, no money, and seemingly no way to take out two to three weeks for a festival. Both finding the money and finding a babysitter were significant challenges for me! I had to decline the invitation.

Several years later I was teaching a summer-school class in music history at the local college. I asked the department chair for money to take students to this festival in Eugene and he agreed to help fund the trip.

When I arrived and heard the quality of the music that was being performed I was astounded. I couldn't believe that a lack of resources had forced me to miss all this great music! I determined that somehow I was going to make enough money so I could be a part of this annual event.

At the festival I met Helmuth Rilling, the conductor and artistic director of the festival, who came to Oregon for this event from Stuttgart, Germany. He is one of the leading experts on J. S. Bach in our time.

After I got acquainted with him I shared with him my dream to make enough money in a business venture to give scholarships to young conductors from other nations, so they might

172

come to this festival and learn from him, and associate with other musicians in such an incredible musical environment.

He was very kind and said, "Tell me when it is the right time."

It took me three years to put together sufficient money, but what a joy it was to me when I was finally able to sponsor a young man from Ukraine to the festival. I have given a scholarship to the festival every year since, sometimes two in a year.

Helmuth conducted workshops all over the world, and the musicians I sponsored were ones that he "discovered" in his travels and recommended for a scholarship. I had the privilege of meeting these musicians in Oregon, and in most cases, helped them buy musical scores that they could take home with them.

Helmuth not only taught me a great deal about giving of one's self to others who can't give back, but he showed me the amazing way that music and business could work together.

He also advised me personally at a very difficult time in my personal life to make some healthy choices for myself. I owe him and his family a great deal. I have known their beautiful daughters, Sara and Rahel, since they were very young. I remember so well waking up in their home in Germany and hearing the girls already practicing their instruments. They practiced several hours a day, and eventually, played in orchestras conducted by their father. Their mother also played the flute in these orchestras. Sara and Rahel are still very dear to me, and now, their husbands also.

Over the last thirty-five years of knowing Helmuth and his family, I have experienced the professionalism and love of the Rilling family, and participated in some truly unforgettable musical performances in many nations. I am so grateful to each of them for their contributions to my life.

All of this only happened, however, because I took charge of my own future and created a business that allowed me to combine my musical background and dreams with genuine help to others. I am glad I didn't give in to my sadness over missing the music early on, but went forward and made a business happen so I didn't miss out again!

What is your deepest dream? Start there and use this dream as a motivation to succeed. Work on your dream. Make it happen. You will never regret it. It will be the ANSWER to the question, *"Why build the biggest and best business possible?"*

The Rilling family has been the foremost role model for me when it comes to combining musical excellence with business and family. To people everywhere I say, "It truly is possible to combine the passion of a dream with business and family!"

How to Pursue Significance

There are several things required to achieve significance.

First, you must learn the areas that deeply interest you and motivate you to be WILLING to make sacrificial gifts of your life.

Second, you must recognize that significance is a total-life endeavor—it requires commitment, responsibility, and perseverance. It is a life that gives repeatedly, frequently, and in many cases, daily. Significance is not found in just making a donation of money or goods. It requires a total giving of self.

Third, a life of significance requires that an individual take full responsibility for developing their own ability to rest, refresh, and recharge themselves—physically, emotionally, mentally, and spiritually—and neither expect or insist that others serve their need for leisure or luxury.

Fourth, a life of significance is a life that seeks to bring about real and lasting CHANGE—it may be political change, social change, spiritual change, economic change, attitudinal change. Whatever the change being sought, there must be real changes in behavior that are manifested and that can be measured or defined.

In summary then, a life of significance is:

- Rooted in your deepest passions and interests
- A total-life endeavor requiring commitment, responsibility, and perseverance
- A life that demands periodic "recharging" in order to serve at maximum ability
- A life that produces real and lasting change

The person who seeks to have a life of significance is *not* a person who can be all things to all people at all times. Rather, the person who seeks to be significant must inevitably focus his or her activities on that one main passion that causes her heart to race, or her blood to boil—that causes her dreams to soar or her sense of justice and injustice to rise up within her.

Beginning at Home. Very few people who are pursuing a significant life began at the international level. Very few people zoom to the top of any profession, or any area of service. Even fewer become known *in a day* for their integrity, reputation as servant-leaders, or for being inspiring role models. And frankly, those who gain quick celebrity status based upon one or two outstanding performances in a well-publicized field of work *rarely* seem to maintain an image of quality "giving" to the world for very long. Perhaps the reason for this is that celebrity status is not earned as much as it is bestowed by loyal fans—and fans for the most part tend to be very fickle, here-today-and-on-to-someone-else-tomorrow people. I am speaking, of course, of those who are fans of particular individuals—usually stars on the silver screen or daily television programs, or on sports courts or fields.

How long did it take Mother Teresa to be recognized as a worldwide person leading a truly significant life? Well ... it took a *lifetime*.

How long did it take for Winston Churchill to be recognized as a significant world leader? It took decades.

How long did it take for Charles Wesley to gain international notoriety as a preacher of the Gospel? Again, it took decades and thousands upon thousands of miles traveled by horseback.

Most lives of significance begin at HOME.

For me personally, there is no more fulfilling life than to raise a family in today's world—helping each person in the family to grow into the person he or she has been uniquely designed to be. I felt this way about my children. I feel this way now about my grandchildren.

Moving Outward to Your "Team." The person of significance also exhibits the qualities of sacrificial giving, focused commitment, and an attitude of service to her "community"—which may be defined as her work team or company, her church or faith community, or her neighborhood.

As these spheres of influence and giving grow greater, a life of significance may be extended to ways of serving the broader community—perhaps volunteering at a local hospital, community center, or working with at-risk children.

At some point, a person who experiments with giving her time and talents in various areas of service will find the one project or cause that truly "clicks." A task will no longer be a task—it will become a *passion*.

Motivating Others to Join You. Eventually, a person of passion will attract others to her cause. She will inspire others to earn more so they can give more, to spend an increasing amount of time in service, and to recruit even *more* associates to an area of significant contributions to the world.

I know a woman who *hates* trash. From her perspective, trash is anything that is *not* in its proper place, and is disruptive or detrimental to the health or safety of others in the broader community. She probably wouldn't be too concerned if your office was cluttered, but she has nothing good to say about a community that is teeming with used bottles, cans, or containers of any type, piles of paper and boxes that are blown helter-skelter across streets and public spaces, and used food containers that attract all sorts of insects and vermin. Her concern is based upon her understanding that trash *can* be discarded in appropriate ways.

There are a couple of key concepts in the paragraph above. My acquaintance does not advocate that every person refrain from producing trash—that would be unrealistic. Her goal is to see people *dispose* of their trash in hygienic, beautifying ways.

In most cases, that means having trash cans readily available, and trash services provided to empty those trash cans.

It means modeling good anti-littering behaviors, and teaching children to clean up the world around them.

She further sees this as "good business." She knows intuitively that people *like* shopping at places that are clean and tidy, whether they are purchasing fast-food meals or buying luxury items or attending concerts or theatrical events.

Few people know or remember that when Walt Disney first founded Disneyland in Anaheim, California, he insisted as a major policy—to both his employees, and as a promise to his investors—that Disneyland would not be like other amusement parks in the southern California area. It would be a clean, family friendly, and fun place *without trash*! The budget for Disneyland, for decades, had as its biggest line item of expense: maintenance. That meant people to sweep the public walkways, clean the eating areas and restrooms, and keep the park freshly painted and pleasing to the eye.

My friend's passion *against trash* took root in her family and neighborhood, but before long, it became a policy in the company where she worked, and eventually, in the company she *owned*. She got her company to purchase trash receptacles that had her company logo on them, along with the words, "We really do *care* about your world." She called it practical advertising. She made certain that the trash receptacles were washed out weekly and emptied as often as necessary.

And then came the next level in the anti-trash campaign. She made "clean up your mess" a well-known slogan throughout her state, and then neighboring states. She began *manufacturing* trash receptacles that could be transported readily to other nations. She gave lectures in overseas meetings showing PowerPoint presentations that "compared" meeting venues that were clean with those that were trashy, and she had the financial statistics to back up her claim that people *wanted* to attend meetings at clean conference centers, and *didn't* return to trashy, filthy ones. She got the attention of major companies in major cities.

Did she singlehandedly eliminate all trash from the planet? No.

Did she make a significant difference in elevating awareness of the issue and motivating people to discard their trash in ways that didn't litter highways, parks, and public areas? YES.

Did she do something that made the world a little more gracious, healthful, and beautiful? YES.

She certainly influenced me!

I like clean places. For many years when I went into a public ladies room, I have found myself cleaning up the floor, the basins, the counter. I wanted the room to be nice for the next women who come in. Of course I know that I don't *have* to do this. But I almost can't help myself. I want things done well.

I don't mind admitting that when I first visited the Taj Mahal with some of my business leaders in India, I was appalled at how filthy the grounds were. The building itself is gorgeous, but there was trash everywhere around it. I just started picking it up! The Indian business leaders looked at me in amazement. I responded, "This is your most prized and sacred place. It must be clean!" They began to help me pick up trash but we faced a second problem—there were no trash cans in which to deposit the trash.

Meet Tera

Tera grew up in a troubled home. Her parents divorced and she struggled living with her mom, who often wanted to end her life. Finally, Tera was sent to live with her dad when she was a teenager. That was very difficult for her. Her aunt intervened and took her to church where she encountered God for the first time. Her life changed, and she eventually was reunited with her mom and she survived.

Tera's advice to young women is resolute: "Get a higher education degree if possible. Be aware of, and engage potential mentors in life. Look into your heart to find the things that you are built for, not what others may tell you to do with your life. Seek authenticity in others and yourself. Be yourself!"

Tera built a successful graphic design business. Now she travels extensively in her business, often to troubled areas helping women get out of slavery and trafficking. She is quick to say, "When God stirs up your heart over something, it is for a reason … look for the action."

Tera did NOT let her upbringing keep her from pursuing her passion and achieving a life with BOTH success and significance!

Challenging Others to HELP Others
Live a Higher Quality of Life

One of my main goals *wherever I go in the world* is to challenge people I meet—in small groups and large audiences, to join me in helping others live a higher quality of life than they are presently living. This is a life of "significance" for me! It has led me to pursue a variety of ventures.

The Pune Baths. I have traveled to India many times. For more than ten years I went there several times a year. One of my great joys in returning home from India was always to take a bath with lots of hot water and bubbles in my own big bathtub! I luxuriated in that bath, but also was acutely aware that a woman in Pune slum in India had never experienced such a bath. There are about five thousand people living in a three-block area in Pune—many of them living in tiny little shacks sometimes stacked three levels high. They have no toilets and no running water.

It took me years but eventually I made a connection with a group at World Vision, and they submitted plans to me about how we might build some bath houses and toilets close by this slum. It took about a year to get the project completed after it was begun, but the day came when World Vision sent me photographs of women with big smiles on their faces as they used the showers and other facilities there. It was a big dream come true for me!

Helping Just One Family. Sometimes entire neighborhoods or regions cannot be helped. But there's nearly always one family that can be helped.

In one of my business groups in India, we had a wonderful opportunity to help a family who had a little girl in need of medical attention. This little girl had spinal meningitis and our entire business team came together, chipped in for transportation, and took care of the rest of the family while the parents went with their daughter to get the medical help she needed. How proud I am of *business* associates who take on concerns like this!

The World Has Untold Orphans. There are literally tens of millions of orphans around the world. You and your close associates may not be able to help them all. But you certainly can find a way to help some of them!

While I was doing business in Cape Town, South Africa, a leader in my business group told me about an orphanage where he volunteered his time. We took a small team to visit the children and see how we might help. These were AIDS orphans. The orphans were grouped together in twenty houses, with about eight to ten orphans of various ages living in a house with a widow who was their "mom."

One ten-year-old girl told me she dreamed of being a singer and she asked me if she could sing for me. She sang, "I believe I can fly, I believe I can touch the sky." We walked down the complex sidewalk singing together.

Later, we were able to provide shoes for all of those children through the generous help of a woman named Bonnie who lived in Hawaii. She heard me speak and asked what she could do to help.

I told her these orphans cannot attend school unless they have uniforms and shoes. She gave me a large amount of cash to supply this need. Imraan, our group leader and his team drew patterns around the feet of the children to get their shoe sizes.

Bonnie later arranged for more than a hundred of these children to go on a cruise ship in the Cape Town Harbor. The captain spoke to the children and said, "If you will work hard in school and get good grades, I will hire you to work on the ship." Many dreams began that day.

My business leaders in Germany saw the commitment we were making in Cape Town and asked what they might do. We had been contacted by a retired dentist in Cape Town who said he was willing to do dental work for the children, but he needed help purchasing supplies. The German group collected enough money for a year's worth of dental materials and for this dentist to hire an assistant. More than two hundred children received dental care for the first time in their lives!

Who Else Might You Help?

I ask people everywhere I speak, including *myself*, this prevailing question: "Who *ELSE* might you help?"

I frequently have asked this question of people who have said to me, "We're just doing okay," or, "We're just fine."

I know that if a person is doing "just okay" or is "just fine," they really aren't doing all that they COULD do to build their business, and if their business is not actively growing, then there are people they know who are *not* doing just fine. The more people they will actively seek to recruit, the more people they will help financially.

If you are doing "just okay" or "just fine," then you aren't maximizing your own potential! You aren't on a rise to something better. And, you aren't pulling up others in your wake toward an overall greater prosperity or level of accomplishment.

This is not only true in business. It is true in every area of life. Show me someone who is helping educate those in her community who cannot read or do not speak English well, and I'll show you a person who is going to make personal friends, generate new customers for whatever line of business or work she is in, and who can help raise the entire water level of financial prosperity in her neighborhood or city.

Show me a person who is NOT content with being "just okay" in her health, and I'll show you a person who is likely going to a gym or a spa—and who will she encounter there? Other people who are also trying to improve their health. Conversations begin. Mutual motivational help is exchanged. Friendships begin to be forged. Relationships forged will nearly always have some sort of business dimension. And, encouragement will nearly always result in people becoming more productive and more energetic in their careers. The information exchanged may help others become more efficient and smarter in their promotional or marketing efforts. New ideas will emerge. And on it goes.

If a person is content to sit down at the current level of success, that level of success may continue for a while, but it will eventually begin to decline.

Those who build vibrant businesses are not "just fine" or "just okay" people. They are willing to take on the struggle, stress, and difficulties of building a business because they want *more*—not necessarily more for themselves personally, but nearly always *more* for their children, their extended family, and their friends. They have a "cause" that drives them that isn't selfish. In most cases, it is a noble cause that produces benefits that are both tangible and intangible!

Significance in Showing Love

Love is another word for *giving*. Those who love, give. And the greatest significance I know comes when we give others a message of love.

There are so many ways to express love—actually, hundreds of millions of ways and more!

Love comes in small gestures, often inexpensive and sometimes random.

I once was given a large box of delicious Belgian chocolates. It was Valentine's Day and I was passing through New York City on my way to an island in the Caribbean. I gave some of my chocolates to a man and his wife who drove me from the airport to the yacht that was my "home" for a few days. When I left the Caribbean a few days later, I still had about half the box of chocolates, so I left the box for this couple with a thank-you note.

Four months later, this man saw me at a meeting and walked straight to me and said, "I ate every one!"

Stop to think about it. That gesture cost me nothing. The chocolates had been a gift to me. I simply passed on a gift, and only half a gift at that. But the gesture was priceless to the one receiving the chocolates. Why? Because it was a sign of my appreciation.

Another time in my life I had the simple opportunity to give a "song" to a woman as an expression of my love.

When my Aunt Ethel, my beloved mentor and great aunt, was ninety-six, she was near death and the doctors said she was in a coma. I went to see her and she didn't respond to my being there. So I went into her living room, sat down at her piano, and began to play. Then I returned to her room to say goodbye. She sat straight up and said, "You are Beverly! Do you know how much I love you?"

I had a chance to tell her one more time what she meant to me.

How grateful I was that she *heard* the message of love I so wanted to convey. I am thoroughly convinced that the people you love *will* hear your voice, even if that person is in a coma.

Love *always* has a healing effect. It is *always* significant.

But those you love need to *know* of your love. And often, they can't or won't know the depth of your love unless you put your love into words, perhaps even a song.

I am a hundred percent convinced that the expression of LOVE, in whatever form you choose to give it, will always be filled with significance. To the person receiving … and to you the *giver*.

CHAPTER 12

Going Global

*BOOTSTRAPPING:
AN ENTREPRENEUR
STARTING A COMPANY
WITH VERY LITTLE CAPITAL

"How wonderful it is that nobody need
wait a single moment before
starting to improve the world."

Anne Frank (1929–1945)
German Jewish Diarist

Anne Frank, quoted above, died in a concentration camp during World War II, but her words live on and ring true even today.

Global is a popular word in our culture today—we hear and read a great deal about the "global village," "the global marketplace," "the global challenges," and about taking advantage of "global opportunities" or pursuing a "global initiative."

Even the person who is establishing a small personal business is wise to raise her sights and broaden her mind to think "global." Why? Because she *can*!

Technology has made the entire world just a click away. Just a short plane ride can take a person just about anywhere. Vast opportunities are within reach.

Several years ago, I found myself thrust into international business in a way that was not entirely my own ambition or choice. Nevertheless, once the international stage was set before me, I decided to step out onto it.

Much of my time in the early part of this current century was spent in international travel, all of it related to business, not vacation. I learned to work on planes, sleep on planes, and forget about time zones unless they dictated the start of a business meeting or the schedule for the next flight.

Below is a summary overview of my itinerary for just one year (2004).

January 31	Johannesburg
February 6	Malawi
March 17	Tampa, Florida
March 17	Washington, D.C.
March 24	London
April 14	London
April 17	Stockholm
April 19	Oslo
April 20	London
May 8	Patna
May 9	Delhi
May 28	Stuttgart
May 30	Salzburg
June 15	Stockholm
August 18	Frankfurt
August 22	Oslo
August 25	Gothenburg
September 25	Cape Town
September 30	London
October 25	Beijing
November 1	Shanghai
November 8	Washington, D.C.
November 16	Kiev
November 25	Runnymede, England
December 12	Maui

Starting my business career after being a college music instructor didn't prepare me for a schedule of this magnitude!

And yes, Maui in December was a work-related conference, although I do admit to a few days of sitting and staring at the ocean.

"It all sounds so exciting!" a few people have said to me.

From my perspective, it was both exciting *and exhausting*. And much of the time, exhausting trumped exciting. I was opening or reinforcing business markets in each of the locations listed above, which meant meeting new people, dealing with ever-changing currency exchanges, and learning as quickly as possible the cultural norms of a place and its people so that I didn't make major communication errors, whether dealing with clients, colleagues, or customers.

I say all of that to say this: International business is never going to be easy. It will always be a challenge!

The Opportunities Are Tremendous. Why move into the international realm? For the same reasons to stay out of it—it is *challenging*. Your mind and heart will be challenged in ways you have never experienced before. Your business abilities will be stretched and developed in exciting ways. The people you meet will enrich your life— mostly for good, I believe.

Plus, there is huge money to be made internationally.

Most businesses I know that have "gone global" have found that, before long, the global side of their business is much larger than the domestic side. I remember being in the elevator of a major hotel in India. I began talking to a representative of Microsoft who told me he was recruiting people there for Microsoft. Later on I understood, but at the time I was quite surprised.

My dear friend and mentor, Bernice, started a health-based business with her husband many years ago. After he died she carried on by herself for decades. Her business went global and is still prospering. She called me one day and said: "Beverly, do you want to go to St. Petersburg with me?" I said, "Sure, I haven't been to that part of Florida." She quickly replied, "I don't mean Florida I mean Russia." She was always expanding my vision. She gave to many charities and inspired those of us who followed her to do the same.

The Friendships Are Deep. Beyond the financial opportunities, you will find a wonderful opportunity to make friends, and to become something of an "ambassador at large" for the United States.

I sense that there is a common misperception these days that Americans are hated the world over. I have not found that to be true. When we reach out with honest expressions of care and opportunity, we are often welcomed with open hearts and minds. Once a relationship is forged, it can be a lasting bond.

I have business associates in India, for example, whose children call me "Beblly Aunty." That word *Beblly* is their form of Beverly! I am accepted as a full member of their *family*.

My Best Advice as You Go Global

Although I have done business now in many nations, over a period of at least twenty-five years, I do not consider myself an expert on every nation in which I have given business addresses or developed business partnerships.

My overarching advice to you is to learn the historical context that you are walking into! It will be invaluable to you as a preface to what awaits you in a particular foreign market. Do your homework.

Some Principles Seem *Almost* Universal. Three of the key principles I have discovered in doing international business seem to hold true in most of the nations in which I have worked:

• *Everything had to be done in a hurry-up mode.* There was no leisure, either in the means of communication or in attitude.

A group of colleagues and I went to Mexico and spent a week there one day. You read that correctly. We had meetings going on all day and thousands of people were milling about either going into a meeting or coming out of a meeting, eager to sign up and get their paperwork approved, and just getting to the right places at the right time was a real challenge. There was no time to eat or drink, and nobody around to offer takeout food from nearby restaurants.

• *We had to stay flexible—and that included staying calm and staying appreciative.* Even if everybody around us seemed in a panic or seemed to be pushing their way toward the goal they desired, we had to remain the peaceful eye in the midst of the hurricane. And at all times, be quick to say thank you for the good things that came our way.

When it came to the lack of food and beverages we experienced in Mexico, I had one memorable experience that changed my outlook toward the frenzy of the days there. I decided I was going to think ahead and I called room service one night a little after midnight and said, "There are twenty of us working like bees in the ballroom and at ten o'clock—that's about ten hours from now—I want to order twenty croissants and twenty cups of coffee brought to us." The person in room service said, "Si, si, señora, no problema."

The next morning at eleven-thirty we received twenty chicken sandwiches and twenty Cokes. It wasn't what we ordered. But it was what we received—and we chose to be thankful for what we received!

• *People hunger for a CHANCE.* I have encountered thousands of people around the world who want only one thing: a chance. They want a chance at a better life, a better future for their children, a better foundation for security to withstand hard times.

We in the United States take for granted the concept of a "chance." The word *opportunity* is old news to us—we become jaded to the extent of potential that can be ours if we will only reach out and *take* the opportunities all around us.

Stay Flexible and Adjust

There are three areas in which flexibility and adjustment are "MUSTS." Be creative … and be patient!

1. Timelines Likely Need to Be Adjusted. One of the greatest adjustments Americans often need to make in other nations is to think "longer range." Long-range to other parts of the world is much *longer* than it is in the U.S.A. The Asians plan ten years out. The Germans plan five years ahead. Many American companies, in contrast, plan for three months—they often work on a "next-90-days" cycle, with quarterly quotas!

2. Product Lines Likely Will Need Adaptation. I have long been an admirer of the ingenuity and flexibility of McDonald's when it opens regional and foreign markets. Most people who have traveled overseas know that the "menu" of McDonald's is fairly uniform wherever one goes. You can always get a Big Mac! But …

When McDonald's went into Hawaii, they added *rice* to the menu. Everything in Hawaii is served with rice!

When McDonald's went to Seattle, they added clam chowder.

When McDonald's went to France, they served local French wine … and in Germany, they served German beer.

In Japan, they added more pickles, and in Malaysia they served "Dorian" milkshakes. (Dorian is a popular fruit in Malaysia.)

It's *still* McDonald's. Any American would be able to find his or her way around the menu. But it's also McDonald's *adapted* for a greater number of local customers.

Always be on the lookout for the adaptation that works.

3. Certain Policies Likely Will Need to be Altered. I have learned through the years that not everything that works in America will work in an overseas market. Many things do work, and the people in the foreign nations are grateful for a system that is proven, stable, and efficient. In other areas, the American way of doing business is too expensive for them to pursue—they simply don't have the money for the initial cost of goods and promotion.

It is generally to the benefit of the American company to work out a "deal"—if possible!

The bureaucracy is nearly always dealt with *best* by people who live in the nation involved. Which raises another issue—there must be a system in place for the American company to assess the honesty of the people with whom it chooses to do business. The most eager "partner" may not be the most scrupulous partner—and at the outset *especially*, honesty is a necessity.

At all times, it is important for an American investor or "partner" to know what is required, what is going on, and what is being done as the new entity establishes itself like an island in a sea of changing regulations and policies. The company that fails to seek a thorough understanding of *how* business is conducted in another nation is going to be a company that fails, usually sooner than later.

At all times, the international company needs to be respectful of the culture of the people they are seeking as business partners.

Plan to Leave Something Valuable Behind

I am always thankful for the team of people that usually works with me as I make presentations about my business and meet with the leadership that has developed in another nation. There is no way to fully show appreciation to those who give of their time so freely, making the business work, taking the tickets and telling people where the bathroom is located, or answering the same question for the thirtieth time. These helpers make a meeting enjoyable for the new prospect or the worn-out colleague who needs a shot of inspiration.

I am especially grateful for these people when I have the occasion to go to a brand-new market and do what I can to carve out a business niche. When I leave, I usually have very little idea as to whether I have been effective. When I get on the train, wave goodbye, I say a prayer that the people with whom I met will be able to take hold of the concepts and forge ahead. They often seem a little like "orphans" to me—they need a guardian or mentor they don't have.

If I can leave videotapes, audio recordings, or printed materials, I feel somewhat better. At least they have *information* to consult. I leave behind as much product and information as I can and return as soon as the schedule will allow.

Be as Generous as You Can Be

On my first visit to India, I found myself facing an audience of thousands of people, many of whom were skeptical at hearing from an American woman.

My opening line to them was a statement to the effect, "I am here to make a LOT of money."

I could almost feel the entire audience tense up. And then I added, "And I intend to leave it all in India to benefit Indians." The place not only relaxed, but erupted in cheers!

I had a dream of doing something significant for the Indian health-care system, and supporting a children's wing of a large hospital in a major city was part of my plan. I challenged the audience members to join me in doing something that would be of lasting benefit in their own nation, and they rallied to the cause!

The Best Public-Relations Approach. Your best "public-relations" move is this: Treat your potential distributors or clients

193

exceedingly well. I've watched companies provide all sorts of FREE goods and services to the people in the area where they are hoping to establish a new business. As long as the goods and services are truly helpful or desired by the people, the end result is nearly always "BIG SUCCESS!"

Become Co-Workers in Helping the Poor. While there are many poor people in every nation, there are also very prosperous people in every nation. Don't lose sight of that fact. My approach has been this: Seek to help the prosperous people in an area join forces with you and others in helping the poor!

On one occasion in Mexico, I was doing some personal shopping in a fine little boutique store that had unusual leather goods and jewelry. I was enjoying the bargaining process. As I paid for my purchases the owner of this boutique asked me what I did to have so much money for buying items in her store. I told her my line of work and she exclaimed, "Everybody I know in this city is talking about your business!"

And then she said, with great sincerity, "I want the people in my city to be prosperous. We have many poor people here that you probably have not seen and won't see. They need our help. If you will come back, I will make arrangements for you to meet people in my home so you can talk about your business. I have a large home with enough room for four hundred people." I asked her what she wanted in return for that kind of hospitality. She said simply, "Help me help the poor children in this city." As I left the hotel to go to the airport the next day very early in the morning a little girl asked me to buy chewing gum from her. She wasn't begging; she was trying to do a little selling. I gave her all the loose change I had and that bought all the gum she had in her little satchel. I saw a face-to-face example of the "poor children" this store owner wanted to help.

Let me assure you, making an alliance with a woman like that was one of the most significant things I have ever done—not only on the humanitarian level of helping children in need, but also in public relations for my business. When people know that you CARE ... and that you care in practical ways that include their prosperity and *also* the alleviation of need in their city or town ... they become strong allies and tremendous workers.

There was a side story to my boutique experience. After I had made some concrete plans to return to speak at this woman's home, I was approached by a young clerk in the store who said to me, "Señora, I cannot do what the owner will do [referring to the offer of her home to host a large meeting], but my husband and I very much want the chance to build a business like yours. Would you come back and help us, too?"

I must admit, she won my heart. She wasn't asking for a handout. She was asking for information and for an opportunity to work hard, give back to her culture, and develop a business that would be a financial blessing to far more than her immediate family. What wasn't there to admire!

And yes, I went back to help her, too.

Meet Michelle

Michelle is the founder, owner, and CEO for a media company and website focused on women's health. It is called EmpowHER. As is true for many entrepreneurs, she began working at a very young age. Her first job was scooping ice cream and flipping hamburgers at age fourteen in a sandwich shop. Through the years, she worked as a model and later was co-owner of a modeling agency. She has had work experience in direct sales and real estate, worked for several state-level governors and commissioners, and for years was active in public service and philanthropic projects.

Tragedy struck her life, and also gave her what she terms an AHA moment. She needed to have a hysterectomy at age forty-two, and this led to a debilitating illness for more than a year—one that involved twelve different doctors, being placed on nine medications, and in many ways, becoming a "different person." She fortunately had the resources to get help for her medical issues, relieve the pain of her suffering, and get in touch with the right experts. She came to a realization that she was not alone in her experience and that there were thousands of other women who suffered or were potential candidates for similar suffering.

She began EmpowHER in 2008 at her kitchen table. She drew upon the energy and insights she had gained from her own health experience, as well as the corporate and not-for-profit experiences she had gained through the years. Her website is one of the largest women's health websites in the world.

From Michelle's perspective, determination, passion, and drive are everything—but they must be balanced with empathy and compassion. I like what she said to me recently, "Women can be extremely powerful and can rule with a velvet hammer. Women need to embrace who they are and what they are, and truly understand just how powerful they are. I also believe strongly that women need to rally around and support each other, and I have little patience with women who try to pull the ladder away from other women. We need to embrace each other, ask for the help we need, and mentor one another."

She offers these words of wisdom:
1. Never give up.
2. Do not take no for an answer.
3. You can do anything you want if you work hard enough. Nothing of value comes easy.
4. Listen to your intuition.

Bits of Wisdom as You Are "On the Go"

There are a number of "bits" of wisdom I share with you on an if-you-can-use-it basis:

Stay Open to New Methodology. Always keep in mind that there are many ways of doing things—and the people in other nations have had thousands of years of figuring out what works best for them. They may still be open to a new approach, but for the most part, you will need to start with their current approach!

I first learned this when I went with my father on a number of occasions into the interior of Mexico, where he was interviewing men who wanted to come to the United States to work. These men were called "braceros" by us. While there, we lived in a small house with no running water. A man came each day to place a large container of water on the roof of the house so we could take showers. We drank powdered milk and shopped at the local market for vegetables and meat—what an experience that was. I felt immersed in another culture and came away from that experience realizing that there are many ways of doing things other than U.S. methods. I had no idea, of course, how that experience in my teenage years would impact my future.

Seek to Make "Connections." Always stay on the alert around you for possible connections you might make as you travel internationally—for your business, and also in your personal life. Be especially aware of those who are seated next to you—often people who are "assigned" to you or who are not of your choosing.

I was invited to Saddleback Church to hear a presidential campaign debate hosted by Pastor Rick Warren. The debate was between John McCain and Barack Obama. Seated next to me was a businessman from New York who greatly admired Rick Warren for his work in Rwanda. He was a manufacturer of drugs that benefit AIDS patients. I told him of my work in Africa to help AIDS orphans.

While I was there at Saddleback Church, I met Paul Rudatsikira, a young man whose family had been through the genocide in that nation. He was looking for people to return to his country to establish business opportunities and he asked me to go with him. When I spoke to a group of real estate investors and told them that I was going to Rwanda, they asked to go along! We ended up with a group of twenty-five people and while we were in Rwanda, we were invited to meet President Kagame. On the way to his office, his Secretary of State said, "Get him talking about cows. He loves cows." I knew a little about cows. I introduced myself to President Kagame as the daughter of an American dairy farmer. He immediately said excitedly, "You like cows?"—and for the next forty-five minutes we heard all about his cows and their value to his nation and we became friends. Nothing is wasted!

On a plane back from South Africa, I was not able to get my normal business-class seating, so I was in the coach-class section. Seated next to me was Ruth Kavuma, a woman in the Parliament of Uganda. She is a great advocate of schooling for girls and women, and for "girl's supplies" in the schools. We became good friends and discovered that we both are members of Rotary International. She became another great African connection.

Connections seem to come in lots of sizes and countless ways. Years ago, I received a phone call one day from a woman named Cathy in Florida. I was living in California at the time. Cathy had found one of my old cassette teaching tapes at a garage sale and bought it, listened to it, and became so enthusiastic about what she heard that she tracked me down and asked to be part of my business.

I arranged to meet with her on my next trip to Florida and learned that she had hosted more than a hundred foster children in her home over a twenty-year period. At the time of our meeting, she had three children with her. They were from Russia. My tape had been a cast-off at a garage sale, but it was "treasure" to Cathy. And Cathy was a treasure to me! I learned a great deal about Russia and about Russian orphans from her.

Sing and Dance! Music often tears down barriers and makes way for friendship. In Shanghai on one occasion, my sister and I were in the ladies room off a hotel lobby when I heard several women speaking to each other in Hebrew. Sure enough, they were from Israel. I began to sing an old Hebrew song, "Dodi-Li," and they laughed and before we knew it, they began to sing with me and we even did a little circular dance right there in the ladies room!

An American and three Israeli women singing an Israeli song and dancing an Israeli dance in a Shanghai hotel restroom? How cool is that?

Music, by the way, is important in most cultures. Several centuries ago in Europe, if a person was visiting a castle and a dinner was held in the person's honor, the after-dinner entertainment was singing. Parts were passed out and each person was expected to sing his part. The music didn't appear from the bottom of the piano bench. Most of the music was sung a cappella, although sometimes there were instruments. It was a business social requirement—expected *etiquette* to know how to sing, and more specifically, how to sing *your part* in a given song.

That's still true in many parts of the world.

It will help you tremendously to know a few songs that are traditional in the culture where you are seeking to do business.

Be Grateful for Familiar Menu Items. Sometimes the food in other places can be exceedingly "strange."

I remember the first time I saw a menu in South Africa that had been divided into two columns. On the left hand side were items considered to be "comfort food." That's where a person could find pizza and hamburgers (about which one must always ask, "Is the meat in this hamburger *beef*?").

In the right column were items such as crocodile steak, loin of impala, smoked ostrich, and kudu filet.

Sometimes I would experiment. Mostly I stuck to comfort food! I was not there to impress, but to make sure I stayed healthy for the entire trip.

Tap into the Power of a Smile. I was once with my three-year-old granddaughter Skylar in the San Francisco Airport. We encountered an older man sitting in a wheelchair. He had a very sad look on his face. The person pushing him and I stopped in fairly close proximity while we got our travel documents in order.

I turned Skylar's stroller around so she could see this man face-to-face. She smiled at him and I watched as his countenance changed *completely*. He suddenly looked soft and tender, and he smiled back at her with one of the sweetest smiles I have ever seen.

It was a small moment. But it was an important one.

There's somebody who needs a smile from you today—it is the simplest and yet one of the most effective forms of encouragement available to us.

I routinely sit in seat 1A on airplanes. Since first-class passengers often board first, my seat position allows me to look at every passenger as he or she boards the flight I am taking. If a passenger looks back at me I smile as sincerely as I can. And in most cases, I get a smile in return.

Traveling seems so much more "human" when smiles abound.

Get Over Yourself! Travel in other nations can be humbling. Expect that and keep smiling!

I was greeted at the airport in Mumbai, India, with a sign that read:

WELCOME — MS. BANELLY SELLY

It took me a few seconds to realize the sign was for me!

There is absolutely nothing to be gained by getting upset if people in another nation do not give you the respect *you* believe you are owed … or know how to pronounce your name … or care about any of your titles, accomplishments, or personal "needs." Be grateful they have sent someone to pick you up at the airport!

And … keep your sense of humor, especially about yourself.

My plane arrived at the Manila Airport late on one occasion, and I had only one hour before I was expected to step onto a stage and speak. My host picked me up at the airport in a van. Traffic came to an absolute standstill when we were still four blocks away from the venue. I said to the driver, "You look straight ahead and I will change clothes back here, and I'll then get out and walk to the auditorium."

I opened my suitcase, pulled out a big skirt and put it over my head like a tent, and proceeded to get dressed for the event. Four Filipino men were sent to escort me the final four blocks to the meeting. As we hurried along, I was nearly overcome by the stifling heat and humidity, but even so, I felt a cool breeze behind me. I reached back to check my clothing and realized my skirt was tucked up in my waistband. Those four men had a "bird's-eye view" but they were too embarrassed to say anything. There was nothing I could do but pull out the skirt and walk on!

Sometimes you just have to get over yourself.

Embarrassing things are going to happen. They are inevitable. But if you let them stop you, people will only remember the embarrassing moment. If you laugh and move on, people will remember how you handled a personal crisis and be encouraged! The choice is yours.

You're Never Too Old

Jan was a college acquaintance of mine, but it was only as we became friends down through the years after college that I learned what an amazing life story she had.

Jan had an incredibly sad childhood. She was sexually abused at age six by an adolescent neighbor, but she never told anyone about it until her adult years. He mother died from breast cancer when Jan was only eleven years old, and her father remarried a woman who was a single forty-two-year-old who did not like children. Her stepmother was jealous of the fact that she looked like her mother and this woman did as much as she could to stamp out all things related to Jan's mother. She would say to Jan things such as, "You are no good and lazy, just like your mother."

One day when her stepmother was on a critical rampage, Jan said, "Don't you ever say another unkind thing about my mother!" The woman flew into a rage, pushed Jan onto her bed, and then got on top of her and started to strangle her. Jan yelled for her brother and when he came to the bedroom door the stepmother got up and ran from the room.

An aunt, and also a dear friend of Jan's mother, were the main sources of encouragement in Jan's life, and these women often provided food for Jan and her three brothers when their father and stepmother refused to "share" food with them.

When Jan was seventeen years old, she literally ran away from home and went to college. She had nothing to her credit when it came to earning scholarships, but the dean of women at the college had pity on her and made a way for her to get into school. She married while she was in college and she and her husband had three children. Jan made raising them her full-time "work." She also completed her own bachelor of arts degree, but didn't complete her required year to gain teacher certification until after her oldest child went to college. She taught elementary school for almost twenty years and loved teaching. Jan saw herself in the business of "teaching children." Indeed, she was!

A life-changing experience happened to Jan about that same time she began teaching school. In the 1980s, Jan suffered sexual abuse from one of her pastors, and in the wake of that experience, she found herself being introduced more and more as a counselor to women who had been abused by pastors, priests, or rabbis. For more than seventeen years, that was her "business." She gave herself to a strenuous and ambitious schedule of ministering truth and love to hurting women.

I realize that Jan's story doesn't fit the normal mold for this book— but the challenges she faced were very much in keeping with the organizational challenges of many women who are considering a business of their own. Her goals were healing and freedom, which were not unlike the goals of many women I have counseled in business. And the best part of Jan's story is that she is very much LIKE countless women I've met around the world who are seeking a better life for themselves and their families. Jan is living proof that your story isn't over … until it really is over. Jan is just now starting a brand-new chapter in her life.

At age seventy-two, Jan felt God tap her on the shoulder one day and say, "Jan, now you are ready to go to Africa!"

She immediately said to God, "I'm too old." But God didn't seem to hear that excuse. He provided escorts to accompany her to Kenya, where she had been invited to come by a Kenyan pastor and his wife, and to speak to abused women there. She is raising funds to build a rescue center where abused women can go for safety, restoration, and empowerment.

Jan did not give me "tips" but I have taken the liberty of drawing the tips below from her life story because I can see such strong associations between her experiences and those of many businesswomen I've met:

1. When you need counseling, get it. It may be in an area related to your business or an area related to your personal life. Counseling has benefit to the *whole* of a person's life if it is in a safe environment.

2. Never think your story is finished until God says it is finished. There may still be a chapter for you to write!

3. The worst thing that happens to you may be the way in which you will help others *best*.

4. Never let another person abuse you or mis-use you. Squawk loud and long until you gain justice. No matter *why* a person seeks to put you down or control you, don't allow that person to succeed. Dig deep within yourself and choose to overcome the worst that they have done and replace it with the best that you, and *God*, can do together.

Jan is grateful for her loving husband who stood by her during the hard times and coming to grips with the abuse she experienced after they were married. She is grateful for the love and support of her children. And that leads me to a fifth tip:

5. Never stop being grateful for the *good things* and loving people that come into your life. The good *will* ultimately prevail!

I don't know any woman who is totally *incapable* of "going global" in some way, for some purpose, for some length of time. I am thoroughly convinced that if more American women would reach out to women around the world with love, opportunity, purpose, and meaningful friendship, we could make a major change in the perception people have of our great nation, and also do a tremendous amount of old-fashioned GOOD.

My prayer is that this guide to a business for your future will inspire you to make a difference in your world. No one can do it like YOU!

And ... NOW IS YOUR TIME!

Sunday Morning
by Beverly Sallee Ophoff

A hurricane was brewing off the east coast of Australia, and we later learned that we were the only plane allowed to take off that day. The flight was extremely turbulent. I arrived late for the first venue of three weekend speaking events that called for me to be in Brisbane, Sydney, and the Gold Coast. Australia is a big place! Look at a map and you'll see that these three locations are a long way apart. There was nothing on my schedule except speak, fly, speak, fly, speak, and fly—nothing between speaking and flying!

Even given the weather and the long hours of travel, I knew I was supposed to be in each place and felt privileged that I had been invited to speak, especially at the weekend's "spiritual service," where I could say whatever I wanted.

In many places around the world where I have spoken to business-related audiences, my time to speak was on Saturday night. I was honored to fill that premier time slot. But I also began to ask various event planners, "Do you think we could ever have a service or a meeting time on Sunday morning?" Initially, there was little interest in such a meeting. But, over the years, the event planners began to schedule a service time on Sunday morning, which was otherwise an "off-conference time slot." This meant that the speaker did not need to limit what was said to information related to the business plan we were presenting and encouraging others to pursue.

While this time on Sunday morning was rarely called a "worship" or "religious" service, the planners knew and the speakers knew, that what was shared on Sunday morning was related to a speaker's beliefs and values, and was not limited to business principles or opportunities.

I never have felt that I should mix Saturday night and Sunday morning. On Saturday night, I shared what I know works in building a business, and specifically, what worked for me in building my businesses. On Sunday mornings, I shared what I know to work in building a person's spiritual life—and more specifically, what worked in building my spiritual life. I feel very free to share spiritual principles and truths on Sunday morning. In many ways, this book is "Sunday morning." My other books are focused on BUSINESS. This book is focused on the reasons WHY I have pursued building the biggest and best quality business I can.

On this particular trip in Australia, the planners of the event told me later that at the end of my talk, nearly two thousand of the three thousand people who came to the Sunday morning meeting raised their hands to accept Jesus into their lives when that invitation was given at the end of my talk. These people then went into a side room to meet with people to receive additional information about how to continue walking in their newfound faith.

It was a difficult day, in the natural. And one of the most challenging trips I have ever experienced.

In the spiritual realm, it was one of the most humbling and encouraging and meaningful days and trips of my entire life!

A good business pursued diligently and with the right training tools can change a person's life—and in that, change their family life and even the life of their extended family, neighborhood, or nation. A spiritual decision can change a person's eternal destiny—and in that, there is great joy!

And so much more!

From Beverly's Heart to Yours!

This 176-page book has many additional insights into life and business:

The Essence of My Message • My Personal Faith Journey • Forgiveness: The Key to Moving beyond Personal Heartache • Three Major Decisions that Keep Me in Focus • Facing the Challenges of Life—Big and Small • Escaping the Deadly Traps • A Wellspring of Encouragement • A Heart for Others • Accomplish Something So You Can Give Something • Business with a Mission • Influence: Leading from Behind • Standing by the Door

Beverly Sallee Ophoff

Beverly Sallee Ophoff grew up in Texas and moved every few months as the daughter of a U.S. Immigration Service father. She regards this upbringing as giving her a perfect educational model for international business!

Her mother invested in her musical training, which was her "first career." She earned a bachelor of arts degree in piano from Point Loma University, and a master of arts in choral conducting at California State College in Los Angeles. For twenty years she taught in public schools, teaching both choral classes and music history. She also served on the Southern California Vocal Association Board and adjudicated choirs at the junior high and high school levels. She was named an Outstanding Woman in California for Music.

In 1978, she began a marketing business that eventually circled the globe. She became deeply motivated to help people in the under-developed nations where she established family-oriented business opportunities and challenged her business colleagues to help with charitable projects. She became involved in helping orphanages in Cape Town and Johannesburg in South Africa, and also an orphanage and school near Mumbai, India. She helped build a wing on a hospital in Calcutta. In Rwanda she helped provide homes for widows of the genocide. For more than twenty-five years, she has worked with internationally recognized conductor Helmuth

Rilling from the Bach Academy in Stuttgart, Germany, providing scholarships to young conductors and performing in specialty choirs internationally.

In 2010 she received the first Generosity Award given by the Amway Corporation for her humanitarian efforts.

Beverly has published two previous books, available in fifteen languages: *The Positive Charge* and *Hitting the Highest Notes*. She has been cited in Sharon Lechter's book, Think and Grow Rich for Women.

Since 2011, she has been using her influence to combat sex trafficking. Her website, Hope Unchained, is an ongoing source of information and motivation to be alert, warn, and rally support for the fight to end pornography and sex slavery.

Beverly and her husband Arthur divide their time between Oregon and Michigan to be near their adult children and grandchildren.